From
COUNTERFEIT
to PRICELESS

From COUNTERFEIT to PRICELESS

Aubrey L. Scott

XULON PRESS

Xulon Press
2301 Lucien Way #415
Maitland, FL 32751
407.339.4217
www.xulonpress.com

© 2017 by Aubrey L. Scott

All rights reserved solely by the author. The author guarantees all contents are original and do not infringe upon the legal rights of any other person or work. No part of this book may be reproduced in any form without the permission of the author. The views expressed in this book are not necessarily those of the publisher.

Printed in the United States of America.

ISBN-13: 9781545618707

Contents

Chapter 1   Caught up and looking for a way out 1
Chapter 2   It feels good, and it feels right 15
Chapter 3   It's time for a decision 30
Chapter 4   Playing games and stressed out 44
Chapter 5   You're marked and set up, now go 54
Chapter 6   Unexpected or expected help is good 70
Chapter 7   Going from completion to a new
            beginning 78

Foreword

This dramatic journey will take you into the life of Brice Realton, an ordinary guy with an extraordinary destiny. Unfortunately, he has to go through hell and high water up to his neck before he can recognize just what that is. With a girlfriend who can't handle rejection and a past that catches up to him, Brice finds himself beaten down and put into a situation that causes him to lose sight of who he is and almost prevents him from finding out who he is to become. From being caught up and feeling good to making sudden decisions and stressing out, this story will make you ask yourself just how bad it can get for one person. With scandal and an undercover government operation gone bad, this page-turner is filled with drama after more drama, uncertainty, and dilemmas of all sorts, until an unforeseen transformation takes place and makes it all worthwhile. Sit back and enjoy.

Acknowledgements

I would first like to thank God for giving me the gift of writing. I know that without him I would not be able to do anything, but with him, I can do all things.

I dedicate this book to all the people who have been an inspiration to me, the people who prayed for me, the people who blessed me in more ways than I can remember, the people who have spoken prophecy into my life, and the people who told me that I should never give up, and always give it to God.

I also dedicate this book to my God sent angel, Charlotte, who I am so proud and blessed to have in my life. Lastly, I want to thank my very awesome daughter, Breeanna Lanae, whom has been my inspiration from the start.

Chapter 1

Caught up and looking for a way out

*T*he day was going pretty good at first for Brice and the fellows. They had just come back from the concert and were looking forward to going to the after-party at the American Legion nightclub. Unfortunately for Brice, he had no idea that there would be drama headed his way. He met up with Adam and Rudolph at Eric's place, where they all planned on leaving together. On the way out, they met Trisha. She was Brice's girlfriend, and she did not look pleased to see him. Brice and Trisha had been dating for four months, and the relationship was headed nowhere fast. Brice had decided that he wanted to go back to Houston, where he grew up, so that he could start his life over. The only problem was that he had planned on doing it solo. He had just gotten approved for a job transfer and was looking to leave in a few months. Apparently, Brice forgot to tell Trisha about it, or maybe he just had no intentions on doing so. Either way, Trisha was not happy to have found out through the grapevine.)

Trisha. So where are you going?

Brice. Well, we are going out, if you really must know.

Trisha. I don't think that you should go out tonight, because we need to talk.

Brice. What you think does not matter anymore, so I suggest you just go back home.

Trisha. I am not going anywhere until we talk about this. Eric. Man, I'm ready to go. Brice you coming? Brice. What do you think?

Trisha. No, he's not coming!

Brice. Look here, Trisha. This isn't cool, so I'm going to tell you one more time. Take your butt home!

Adam. Oh no!

Trisha. I'm not going anywhere until you tell me that you are taking me with you.

Brice. No. It's just the fellows tonight, but it's a free country.

Rudolph. I don't think she's talking about the club, bro.

Brice. I know you're not talking about Houston!

Trisha. Why not? I thought that you loved me.

Brice. Who told you that? (The fellows laughed.)

Trisha. You did, right before you made love to me. I know that you won't admit it in front of your boys, but you know that it's true.

Brice. This relationship was over before it even started. I didn't love you then, and I sure don't love you now.

Trisha. I don't believe you. What about Kira and Dre?

Brice. This is not about them. This is about you and me, and right now, there is no you and me.

(Trisha cried as she pushed Brice.)

Trisha. You're not leaving without me, because the Lord told me that you are going to be my husband.

(All the fellows laughed.)

Brice. You crazy girl. It will be a cold day in hell before I marry you, and that's my word.

(All the fellows laughed again.)

Trisha. You laughing now, but just watch. You're not leaving without me, and that's the truth. Brice. Any way. Bye!

(The guys got in the car and drove off to the club. For some reason, Brice could not have a good time. He had never experienced anything like that before, and it somehow made him a little uneasy about the whole situation. He could not stop thinking about it.)

Eric. Man, you need to relax. Here, have a drink.

Brice. No thanks.

(For some strange reason, Brice started to think about Kira and Dre. See, Brice had a good relationship with the kids, and he didn't realize how much it would hurt them to see him leave. You see, Brice was ready to have kids of his own, just not with someone like Trisha. All he wanted from her was sex, but it was so good to him that he ended up meeting her kids. They instantly fell for him, especially Kira. Their biological father had left them, and they really needed a strong role model in their lives. Brice started to think about how he could still have a relationship with the kids without being involved with their mother. It was impossible for him to do so. So Brice decided that he would just have to say good-bye to all of them. The next day, Brice went to see the kids to tell them that he was leaving soon, but before he could open his mouth, Kira greeted him.)

Kira. Hey, Mr. Brice. Are we moving to Houston? (Apparently, Trisha had already told the kids about the move but decided to include them.)

Brice. Yeah, I'm moving to Houston. That's what I came over to tell you.

Kira. What about us?

Dre. Yeah. Are we going too?

Brice. You can come to visit if you like.

(Kira began to cry and ran out the room, while Dre started to tear up and looked down at the floor. Brice was sad and didn't know what to say. He was furious at Trisha and demanded that they went in her room to talk about this.)

Brice. What were you thinking?

Trisha. I told you already. You are going to be my husband.

Brice. Have you been doing drugs? Don't you know that it will never work?

Trisha. Yes, it will. I will do better, and I will give you what you want.

Brice. No, you won't. You don't have it in you.

Trisha. I can try. Besides, you know that you want me.

(Trisha started to try to seduce Brice, and he tried to resist, but that was one thing he couldn't do.)

Brice. What are you doing?

Trisha. I'm giving you what you want baby, and you know that you want this.

(This was one area that Brice couldn't resist, so he fell prey to her seduction. After all, this was what he liked most about her.)

Trisha. Baby, you are very good with my kids, and they love you.

Brice. I love them too.

Trisha. I think that you are the perfect father figure for them, and you would make a great father as well. I'll give you one if you want.

Brice. Really?

Trisha. Of course I will! I love you, and there is nothing that I wouldn't do for you.

(Brice reached for a condom out of Trisha's nightstand, but Trisha whispered in his ear while caressing him.)

Trisha. Let's make a baby, sweetheart. Your baby.

(Brice then dropped the condom and then proceeded to make love to Trisha. He enjoyed it even more than he had normally done but did not seem to realize what he was doing. Not only had he risked exposing himself to something, but he might be making a baby with the one woman he had been trying to leave. A few weeks went by, and things seemed to have gotten a little better between the two of them, but this was not enough for Brice. From time to time, he would remember how stubborn and jealous that Trisha could be. She was too controlling and didn't know how to shut up sometimes, but on the other hand, he also remembered how kindhearted she could be, and the sex was so good to him that he wished that a marriage could be built on top of it. Unfortunately for Brice, this whole idea of trying to do what was right just made him confused. So he concentrated on other things. For instance, Michelle, an ex-girlfriend, had recently gotten in touch with him. She invited him to come up to Chicago for a visit. Brice thought this was a great idea, considering what he was dealing with. So he explained it to Trisha, hoping that she would back away from the idea of them being together. He was amazed when she told him that she would wait for him.)

Brice. Trisha, I'm going to see if we still have feelings for each other. That doesn't bother you?

Trisha. Of course it bothers me, but if that's what you must do, then do it. We will be right here when you get back.

(Brice really didn't understand why Trisha was being so understanding about the situation, but he wasn't going to stay and try to find out either. Brice told Michelle that he would be up there sometime around the Christmas holiday. He had already made sure that he shopped for gifts for Kira and Dre. Before leaving, Trisha called Brice from her job. She got his voicemail.)

Trisha. Honey, can you please stop by my job after you get off work? I have to talk to you about something very important. (Brice checked his voicemail during lunch, and reacted to the message.)

Brice. Damn it to hell! I knew something was going to mess things up for me. What does she want now? (When Brice got off work, he immediately went to see Trisha.)

Brice. So what is so important?

Trisha. Have a seat.

(Brice sat down but was looking at Trisha like he knew what she was going to say.)

Brice. Let me guess, you realized that you may lose me, so you don't want me to go. Right? (Trisha smiled.)

Trisha. No, that's not it, but you are welcome to guess again if you'd like.

Brice. What do you mean that's not it? That has to be it. What else could it be?

Trisha. I'm pregnant.

(Brice sighed and paused for a few seconds.) Brice. Damn it to hell! Why is this happening to me?

Trisha. You wouldn't understand. I told you that you are going to be my husband.

Brice. You no-good skank! How could you stoop so low?

Trisha. Wait a minute, honey. You knew what you were doing, and no one made you do anything that you didn't want to do.

Brice. You tricked me, and I know what you're trying to do; but that is not going to work.

(Brice stormed out of there and did not see Trisha or the kids until it was time to leave for his trip to Chicago. He dropped off the gifts for the kids, and then he left. Trisha tried to get him to stay, but he was still very upset with her. On the way to Chicago, Brice was feeling a little nervous about things. He could not stop thinking about Trisha being pregnant, but he tried to block it out anyway. He arrived at Michelle's place the night before Christmas Eve. Once he got there, he realized that he didn't get her a Christmas gift, so he thought that he would take her out to a nice restaurant. Michelle met Brice outside and greeted him with a hug and a kiss on the cheek. Brice was very pleased with how she had looked. She had a petite frame and a very pretty face, as if she were a model. And she had the cutest crooked smile he had ever seen.)

Brice. Hey, you look very nice.

Michelle. Thank you, handsome. You're not bad yourself. So how was your trip?

Brice. It was longer than I thought it would be, but it definitely was worth it. The traffic wasn't that bad either.

Michelle. Well, that's good to hear. You should be tired. You want to rest for a while?

(Brice was exhausted from his very long day in general, but he was excited to see Michelle.)

Brice. I am a little tired, but I'd rather talk to you for a while.

Michelle. Okay, but let me know if you want to rest for a while.

Brice. Okay.

Michelle. I didn't think that you would come all the way up here, but I figured that I had nothing to lose by asking. My mama taught me that I should never be afraid of rejection. I guess I learned something from her after all.

Brice. I'm glad that you called, because I was hoping to get the chance to spend some time with you. It has been a while, you know.

Michelle. I know? Too long.

Brice. So where is the little cutie at?

Michelle. She is sleeping right now, but we can go and check on her. (Both of them go to look in on her.)

Brice. What's her name?

Michelle. Lori Marie.

Brice. That's a nice name, and she looks just like you.

Michelle. Really? Cause I don't see it.

Brice. Of course she does. She has your head and your complexion. I can't see her eyes, yet, but it looks like she has your pretty lips too.

(Michelle blushed but couldn't help but remember how she had hoped Lori could be for Brice. Apparently, Brice and Michelle had met up awhile before Lori was conceived, but after Brice left, Lori met an older guy that was pursuing her pretty hard. It had been a few months since Brice had left, and Michelle ended up getting caught up in the moment with the guy. Sounds like someone else we know. It was ironic how they both found themselves in such sticky situations, but the fact remained that they both had a child that they had to take care of. At least according to Trisha.)

Michelle. So what's up with you? Are you still seeing that girl from New Orleans?

Brice. Yeah, kind of.

Michelle. What does that mean?

Brice. I was actually trying to break up with her a couple of months ago, but she wasn't hearing it.

Michelle. What is so hard about it? All you have to do is break it off. That's if you really want to.

Brice. It's not that easy. She has these two wonderful kids, and I have grown attached to them. Especially her little girl.

Michelle. I know you're not staying with her because of them. Don't you know that a lot of women try to keep their men by using the kids? Even if the man isn't their father.

Brice. Yeah, I know, but when I tried to tell the kids that I was moving back to Houston, they thought that they were coming with me.

Michelle. How is that?

Brice. Their mama told them that she was going to marry me and that all of us were moving.

Michelle. Now that was dirty.

Brice. I know, but that made it harder for me.

Michelle. You fell for that?

Brice. That is only half of the problem. Before I left, she told me that she was pregnant.

Michelle. Oh my! And you think that you're the father?

Brice. I don't know what to think. All I do know is that this confuses the hell out of me.

Michelle. What are you going to do?

Brice. I really don't know right now, but I don't want to talk about it anymore.

Michelle. Why don't you go lie down for a while? I'm going to fix some dinner. You are hungry, right?

Brice. Yeah. That sounds good, but wake me up, as soon as the food is ready.

Michelle. Okay.

(While Brice went to take a nap, Michelle thought about how much Brice loved barbecue chicken and baked macaroni with cheese. While cooking, she was trying to figure out how she could convince Brice that he would be better off there with her. Michelle talked to herself.)

Michelle. I can't believe this. I am not going to let that ghetto trailer trash tramp, hold on to the one man that I knew would be with me. Now that he is where I'd always hoped he should be, there is no way that I am going to lose him this time.

(It took no time for Brice to fall asleep. He was really exhausted from everything that has been going on. Dinner was ready after about two hours. Michelle took out a bottle of wine that she had bought just for the special trip. She woke Brice and told him to freshen up for dinner. Brice smelled the aroma from the kitchen and smiled, then quickly got himself together.)

Brice. Wow, that smells great! What are you trying to do? Spoil me already?

Michelle. I never stopped, remember? That was your decision to go our separate ways.

Brice. You know, I really don't know why I did that, but I do know that it was very foolish of me.

Michelle. Yes, it was, but that is the past, and I have moved on. At least we can be friends again.

Brice. Yeah. Who knows what can happen, right?

Michelle. Right. Anyway, eat something. I know you must be pretty hungry. Hopefully I made it just the way you like it.

Brice. It looks great, and I'm sure it tastes great too. (Brice tasted the macaroni and then bit into the chicken. He then smiled.)

Brice. This is very good. I see you still got it.

Michelle. Thank you. I am trying to cook more often now that I am a mother, but not having a man to cook for doesn't help much. Here. Have a drink of wine.

Brice. What's the special occasion?

Michelle. Well, you, of course.

Brice. Me? Well, I don't feel special. LOL. Unless you mean special-ed.

(They both let out a very brief laugh.)

Michelle. You should not stress so much. I am sure that everything will be fine.

Brice. I hope so. You know what? I just remembered that I didn't bring you a Christmas gift.

Michelle. That's okay. You didn't have to. Just having you here is a gift in itself.

Brice. Thanks. That's nice to hear, but I want to get you something. You deserve it. Are there any good restaurants around here? Maybe we can go out to eat tomorrow.

Michelle. Yeah. I know a good one.

Brice. Good. I want to take you there and make up for it.

Michelle. You don't have to do that.

Brice. Yes I do, and I want to. Besides, we haven't been out together in a long time.

Michelle. Okay then. If you insist. How about seafood?

Brice. Anything you want is fine.

Michelle, but it will have to be after we go to visit my mama.

Brice. That'll work. I'm looking forward to seeing your mom.

Michelle. Not as much as she wants to see you. Ever since I told her that you were coming, she has been calling me to make sure that you and I come over there. I'm surprised that she hasn't called since you've been here.

Brice. Well, you know that she and I always did have a good relationship. Is she still cooking a lot?

Michelle. Not like she used to. Oh, I meant to tell you. My mama has a man now.

Brice. Really?

Michelle. Really. And he cooks for her most of the time. I hardly see her since she started dating again. I guess because she thinks that she is young again.

Brice. Mama has a boyfriend, and he cooks for her. I didn't see that coming.

Michelle. That's not all. They go out dancing, and to the casino sometimes.

Brice. What? Now I can't believe that. She never went out when you and I were together.

Michelle. I told you that she thinks that she's young again.

Brice. You're not lying. Well, I'm happy for her. She definitely deserves it. After all, she has dealt with a lot of hard times in her lifetime.

Michelle. I felt the same way as you, but she has taken it too far.

Brice. What do you mean?

Michelle. She is having sex more than I am and then calls me to tell me about it.

(Brice laughed at Michelle.)

Michelle. That's not funny, you know.

(Brice walked up to her and whispered in her ear. Michelle put her

wine glass down.) Michelle. Say that again.

Brice. You heard me. Are you due for a little intimacy?

Michelle. Yes I am, but not just a little. I could actually use a whole lot.

It's not like I'm getting any, you know.

Brice. Good thing I'm here.

Michelle. Oh yeah? Why is that?

Brice. Do you remember the sink?

Michelle. The sink? Oh yeah. Vaguely. You think that you can refresh my memory a little?

Brice. I'm going to do better than that. I'm going to show you how it should have been.

(Brice picked Michelle up and carried her to the bathroom. He sat her on the edge of the sink. Then he began to kiss her on her neck and took her top off. Michelle was in a trance as Brice caressed her. She took off her skirt and tried to get to his pants. They began kissing passionately and seemed to enjoy every moment. Michelle was eager for Brice, but enjoyed the foreplay even more. There was more caressing and kissing, and she couldn't take it any longer.)

Michelle. Make love to me!

(So Brice made love to her on the sink for a few minutes, then he picked her up and took her to the living room. And after a little while, they made their way to the bedroom, where it eventually ended. They looked at each other with a grin on their faces, and they didn't quite

know what to say. Michelle kissed Brice.)

Michelle. Thank you.

Brice. The pleasure was all mine, so I thank you.

Michelle. Well, I don't know about you, but I can sure get used to that.

Brice. Me too. (They heard faint noises.) Michelle. Is that my baby that I hear?

Brice. I think that she heard you first.

Michelle. Ha Ha Ha. You're the one who got my baby thinking that I was in trouble up in here.

Brice. So you got jokes too. Well, you can just call me the happy burglar then. Moms are happy when I break in. Michelle. You can break in here anytime, baby. (Michelle went to check on Lori Marie. The baby cried for Michelle to feed her. After getting her a bottle, Michelle brought her to Brice.)

Michelle. Look at Mr. Brice, baby girl. Say hello, pumpkin. Say hey to Mr. Brice.

(Lori was only six months, but sometimes Michelle would forget.)

Brice. Hello there, cutie. Man, she has hazel eyes.

Michelle. Yeah, she gets them from her father, unfortunately.

Brice. Why do you say it like that?

Michelle. Why do you think? That joker doesn't do anything for her, but he is always trying to get in my panties. I'm not playing that.

Brice. I feel you, but I can see why he would keep trying. Especially after what just happened.

Michelle. Believe me when I say, that fool did not get anything like that, and he never will.

Brice. Okay then. Let's change the subject. So how is the new job going?

Michelle. It's okay, but I'd rather be going back to school to get my masters.

Brice. Why don't you?

Michelle. It isn't that easy to do when you have a very young baby. Besides, I like being a mommy. I just wish that I didn't have to do it by myself. She is going to need a father figure soon, but there doesn't seem to be many good candidates nowadays.

Brice. Well, I've always said that a man should find himself a woman and not the opposite. When the time is right, he will find you.

Michelle. I was kind of hoping that he already did.

Brice. Really? Well, maybe he did, but only God knows who and what is right for you. Just ask him, and I'm sure that he will let you know.

Michelle. Right. And how long am I supposed to wait for an answer?

Brice. I don't know. Believe me, I am not the one to tell you how to do it, but I do know that if we don't wait on him, then things can get a little ugly.

Michelle. Brice, things have already gotten ugly. How can you talk like you're a holy roller when you don't even know how to handle your own ugly situation?

Brice. Wait a minute now. I know I'm not perfect, nor do I profess to be, but people do make mistakes, you know. Besides, you can't talk. It was only a few months after I left that you got pregnant—and with someone you didn't want to be with. Don't try to get my speck out my eye when you clearly have a plank in yours. I think I heard a preacher say that one time.

Michelle. Okay, okay. You're right. I guess we both have something in common then.

Brice. Right. So don't come persecuting me for something that you already done.

Michelle. Okay, okay. I'm sorry. I guess I'm just disappointed with myself, and I kind of took it out on you. What I mean is that I was hoping that you and I would have had a baby.

Brice. That's funny. I used to think the same thing.

Michelle. Really?

Brice. Yeah. Ever since I heard that I might become a daddy, all I could do was ask myself why it wasn't with you.

Michelle. I've been asking myself that too. So what do you think that we should do?

Brice. I can't answer that question. I need time to think.

Michelle. Okay. I know that you will make the right decision. Brice. I really don't know what is right anymore.

(Michelle frowned as she left the room. It looked like her plan was not working, but she seemed eager to want to convince Brice into moving with her instead of going to Houston.)

Brice. Sweetie, I'm going to jump in the shower. Is that okay?

Michelle. Of course. Go ahead.

(A few minutes after Brice went to take a shower, his cell phone rang. Michelle checked to see who was calling. She noticed that the name Trisha was flashing. She was tempted to answer the phone, but she didn't want to upset Brice. The phone stopped ringing after a few rings. She exhaled and thought to herself.)

Michelle. I wonder if that was the tramp that is claiming to be pregnant.

(The phone rang again, and it was Trisha. Michelle took a deep breath, and let it out, then answered the phone.)
Michelle. Hello.

(Trisha was shocked that a female's voice was on the other end. She remembered how Brice would not let her ever touch his phone. Instead of getting ugly, she composed herself.)

Trisha. Hello, may I speak to Brice?

Michelle. He isn't available at the moment. Can I take a message? Trisha. Yes, please. Can you tell him that his baby mama called? (Michelle bit down on her lip with anger.)

Michelle. Excuse me, but Brice doesn't have any kids.

Trisha. Not yet, but he will in about nine months.

Michelle. Really? I didn't know that. I will let him know that you called.

Trisha. Thank you boo!

(After they hung up, Trisha smiled, and rubbed her stomach.)

Trisha. I guess Daddy will be coming home sooner than he thought. We need to be ready for him.

Chapter 2

It feels good, and it feels right

Meanwhile, Michelle's doorbell rang. It was her mother and her mother's boyfriend. Michelle greeted them at the door.)

Michelle. Hey, what are you doing here?

Mom. Is that any way to greet your dear old mama? So where is that handsome son-in-law of mine?

Michelle. In the shower.

Mom. So are you going to invite us in or what?

Michelle. Come in. Hey, Robert.

Robert. Hello there.

Mom. So how was it?

Michelle. How was what?

Mom. You know what, baby girl. That first time in a very long time.

(Her mom let out a brief laugh)

Michelle. Mama, I don't know what you're talking about.

Mom. Oh, really. You must be waiting for later so you can have more privacy. I don't mind watching my granddaughter for a while.

Michelle. Mama, I do not need you to watch my daughter. I am grown, and if I want to have some alone time in my house (Michelle hesitated) then I will just wait until my baby is asleep.

Mom. Baby, why are you so hostile and offensive? I was only trying to help.

Michelle. Well, thank you, but I don't need any help. The three of us will be just fine.

(Just as Michelle said this, Brice was coming out of the bathroom. Michelle gulped, and Brice smiled and acted as if he didn't hear her. Her mom rushed over and hugged him. He blushed because he was half-naked with just a towel.)

Brice. Hey, Mama. I missed you too. How have you been?

Mom. Baby, Mama's been fine, but I'm doing better now that you've come to visit us.

Michelle. Visit me, Mama!

Mom. Well, you know what I mean.

Brice. I did come to see all of you. After all, Mama and I have always been close.

Mom. That's right, baby. You're the son that I've always wanted.

Michelle. Mama, what about Junior and Johnny?

Mom. Baby, those are my sons, but neither of them has the potential that this one has.

Brice. Thank you, Mama. I knew that you cared for me, but not like this.

Mom. Baby, don't thank me. I just hope that the two of you can get it together this time, cause this daughter of mine needs to get married and give me some more grands.

Michelle. Mama, stop!

Robert. Please do, Mary. You might run the fellow off. He just got here, so let him relax.

Michelle. Thank you, Robert.

Brice. It's okay. If my mama was alive today, she would have told me that I was a fool for not being with Michelle. So I can understand why your mama feels the way she does.

Mom. Thank you, baby. See, baby girl, I can't help myself. The two of you are perfect for each other.

Michelle. I know, Mama, but it isn't going to be as easy as you think.

Mom. And why is that? All you have to do is be together. And take care of your little girl.

Brice. Well, Mama, Michelle is right. It's complicated. You see, before I left to come here, I found out that I may be a daddy.

Mom. Oh my, that is pretty complicated. What are you going to do, honey?

Brice. Right now, I do not know. And I'm not here to talk about that, anyway. I am here for something else.

Michelle. Right. Sweetie, why don't you go and put some clothes on while I talk to mama?

Brice. Okay. (Michelle got her mother to sit down for a moment.)

Michelle. Mama, why do you have to be so darn nosey? You know he just got here, and I don't want anything to get in the way this time. So please, I beg you. Let me handle this, okay? I am a grown woman, and I know exactly what I'm doing.

Mom. Well, okay then. Excuse me for caring about you. All I want is to see two people that I believe are destined to be together finally just let it happen, but if I'm out of line, then I will step back and let you handle it, baby girl.

Michelle. Thank you, Mama. I know you mean well, and I do appreciate your efforts, but this is something that I must do for myself. I do love you for all you've done to try to help us to be together, but it's time for you to let me an adult.

Mom. Okay, baby girl. Mama loves you too, but you got your hands full with this one. I hope you two can work things out, no matter what. (They hugged one another.)

Mom. So where is my grandbaby?

Michelle. In her crib.

Mom. Let me go see my sweetheart.

(Just as the bedroom door opened, Lori Marie cried for her grandma. Apparently, she had already heard her voice in the other room.)

Mom. I knew my grandbaby heard my big mouth up in here. Hey, angel. Grandma missed you too. (Lori Marie stopped crying once her grandma picked her up.) Mom. See, my grandbaby misses me too. (Brice comes back in after putting some clothes on.)

Brice. I was telling Michelle how much the baby looks like her.

Mom. Really? I think that she looks like her auntie Faith. Look at those cheeks of hers. And that pea for a head. If I didn't know better, I'd think that Faith had this child.

Michelle. Now we all know that didn't happen, but I do wish that she could have taken the pain for me. It was excruciating. I don't know if I can do that again.

(Brice looked at Michelle with a look of disappointment.)
Mom. Now, baby, what if your man wants another child?

Michelle. That's different, Mama. If I get married, and my husband wants kids, then that's something that he and I, will talk about. Until then, I will give all my love to my precious little girl. (Brice's phone rang just as Michelle completed her sentence.) (He answers.)

Brice. Hello.

Trisha. Hey, sweetie. I was just calling to make sure that you made it there safely.

Brice. Yeah I made it here safely, but I'm kind of busy right now.

Trisha. Okay then. The kids said hello, and they look forward to seeing you soon.

Brice. Well, tell the kids that I said hello also. Bye. (Brice was a little embarrassed by the call, so he turned his phone off.)

Brice. Sorry about that.

Mom. So what kids were you talking about, baby?

Michelle. Mama! What did we talk about?

Mom. It's just a simple question.

Michelle. No, it isn't. That is none of your business, so if you and Robert don't mind, we will be getting ready for bed soon. And it is getting late.

Mom. Okay, Okay.

(Michelle took Lori Marie and put her down in her crib.)

Mom. Son-in-law, it was good to see you. Make sure that you come by and get some of Mama's cooking before you leave now.

Brice. You know I will.

(They hugged, and then Brice and Robert shook hands. Michelle came back out and hugged her mom.)

Michelle. Okay, you guys, be safe going home. I love you, Mama. Mom. I love you too, baby girl. Bye-bye for now.

(Mom and Robert drove off.)

Michelle. I'm sorry that my mama tried to get into your business. She is always trying to tell someone else what they need to be doing. What she needs to do is practice what she preach.

Brice. It's okay.

Michelle. No, it's not okay. She has no right to ask you personal questions like that.

Brice. No, really, it's okay. Maybe I need someone like her to remind me that I do need to get my priorities straight. I have been on my own for a long time. And most of the decisions that I made, I made them with no help. It would have been nice to have somebody to talk to. Cause I didn't have my mom or dad. Or really anyone who I thought genuinely cared for me.

Michelle. Do you think that your mom would have liked me?

Brice. You didn't hear me earlier? My mom would have loved you.

Michelle. Really? Then what happened to us?

Brice. I told you earlier that I don't know. It just happened. I am very sorry for what I did, but I can't erase it. All I can do is tell you that the immature man you met years ago is gone now, but he still has some issues to deal with.

Michelle. What makes you so sure that he is gone? You said that you don't even know what you're going to do about your situation. Brice, I know things are difficult right now, but I have a baby to take care of, and it looks like you might have one too. If we don't get it together for their sake, then these kids might have it just as bad as we did. And I don't want that for my daughter. I will not have her grow up without a father who really can love her the way she needs to be loved. I have loved you for a very long time, but I will not take a chance if you don't know what you're going to do. My daughter means the world to me, and I don't take that lightly. I am here for you, and I will help you in any way I can, but you need to be honest with me. Promise me that you will not break my heart again.

Brice. I promise. Michelle. I love you too, but I really need time to think about things before I make any sudden decisions this time. Been there done that already.

Michelle. I understand. In the meantime, let's sit down and talk about life.

Brice. What about it? It seems to know more about me than I do. I wish things wasn't so difficult. That way, I can do what I want and not have to deal with any circumstances.

Michelle. Where have you been? Don't you know that without risks, there would be no challenges? And life would be boring.

Brice. Well, fortunately for me, my life has been all about taking risks. Whenever I have to decide on something, it seems like there is always some kind of risk involved.

Michelle. Like my biology professor used to say, life is like a box of chocolates. You never know what you're going to get.

Brice. I thought Forrest Gump said that.

Michelle. Did he? Yeah, I remember. He was talking to that lady on the bench. He also said, stupid is what stupid does.

(Brice laughed.)

Brice. I know that's right. He must have been talking about you, right?

(Michelle laughed.)

Michelle. Yeah, but you first. (They both laughed)

Brice. That's okay. I may have fallen for many things in my lifetime, but no more.

(Brice seemed to think that just because he had realized that he had made mistakes, that all he had to do was acknowledge them and then decide to not make them anymore. Boy was he wrong. Michelle and Brice both had a lot to learn about life and all of its bag of tricks. Meanwhile, Trisha was taking her own risks. Without consulting with Brice, she began planning a wedding. The very interesting thing was that there were many people eager to help her out, mostly from the church that she and Brice went to. The pastor had no problem counseling them, once he heard from Brice, of course. And it seemed like everything was going according to her plan. The only problem, which was a big one indeed, was that Trisha apparently had a fling with a guy since she and Brice had been together. The guy was an old friend from high school who had been wanting to get with her for a long time. They obviously had an attraction for each other and started seeing each other on a discreet level, but Trisha cut it off with him around the time she had gotten pregnant. The thing was that she wasn't really sure who the father was, but she decided that it must be Brice since she was with him more. Besides, she thought it was more suitable for Brice to be the father since he was stable and she had loved him. Troy, who was the other man, was convinced that the baby was his for some reason. And he told Trisha that he was going to tell Brice about them, until he found out that Trisha would do anything to keep Brice. For example, she went to Troy's job and caused a scene, which almost got him fired. Then she poured sugar down his gas tank and busted up his windshield and said, "You sure you want to be my baby's daddy?" It didn't take long for Troy to back away and leave her alone. After that, all that was left for Trisha's plan was to get Brice to come back home soon. So she called him up and told him that she was having some complications with the baby and needed him to come back and comfort her.) (This was the following day, and Michelle was at the grocery store.)

    Brice. What happened?

    Trisha. I think that I may have to go to the hospital. My stomach has been cramping up pretty bad, and I need you. I'm bleeding a little also.

Brice. Call your mom to take you. You know that I'm ten hours away.

Trisha. I know, but I will feel better knowing that you were here.

(Trisha began to sob and moan as if she was in more pain.)

Brice. Okay, okay. I will get down there as soon as I can, but still ask your mom to take you, and I will see you when I get back.

(They hung up, and Brice realized that it would hurt Michelle if he left so soon.)

Brice. What am I going to do? Damn it to hell! Why is this happening to me?

(Michelle came in from grocery shopping and noticed that Brice seemed a little on edge.) Michelle. Are you okay?

Brice. Yeah. Why do you ask?

Michelle. Because you look like something is troubling you, that's why.

Brice. I'm okay. I think that I feel guilty for not being there for my child, but I'll be fine.

Michelle. Did that tramp call you again?

Brice. No. I just have been doing some thinking, that's all.

Michelle. I hope that we are in that thinking.

Brice. Of course we are.

Michelle. So have you made up your mind?

Brice. Not yet, but I will let you know soon. I'm going for a walk.

I need some fresh air.

Michelle. Good. I'll come with you.

Brice. No. I want to be alone. I need to think some more. I will be back soon.

(Michelle felt pushed away.)

Brice. I just need some more quiet time, that's all.

Michelle. Okay then. I'll have dinner ready when you come back.

(While out, Brice tried to figure out how he is going to go back to Trisha without hurting Michelle in the process. He realized that there was no way around it. A voice in his head told him to just go because it was the right thing to do. After all, there was no guarantee that a relationship with Michelle would work, because it had been so long since they dated. So he decided that he would just go ahead and tell Michelle that he was leaving. He returned from his walk and found Michelle sitting on the couch. She looked anxious.)

Michelle. How was your walk?

Brice. I'm feeling much better.

Michelle. So you have made a decision then.

Brice. Kind of. I think that I need to go back home for a while and sort some things out. And once I get things straight, I can come back.

(Brice knew that he was not telling the truth but, nevertheless, tried to get Michelle to believe him. He just didn't want to hurt her. Unfortunately, Michelle saw through him.)

Michelle. So you are going back to her! Why did you even bother to come up here in the first place? All you know how to do is just lie and deceive. I don't believe that you could change if you wanted to. (Michelle continued to lash out at Brice.) You can't keep coming in and out of people's lives like this and expect them to understand.

(Brice tried to talk, but Michelle didn't let him get a word in.)

Michelle. I'm sick and tired of being hurt and let down. I might as well be a lesbian!

(Brice looked at her like she was crazy.)

Michelle. At least I don't have to worry about us anymore.

Brice. Why are you overacting? I told you that I will be back, and then we can move on with our lives.

Michelle. Fool, please. You expect me to believe that? Nothing you said to me is the truth. You must think that I fell off a truck full of rocks or something. I'm not waiting on something that's never going to happen. You go back to your little tramp and find out what a big mistake that you're making, but don't call me when you meet karma. Me and my daughter, will be just fine without you.

(Michelle tried to hold back the tears but couldn't help it. She then ran and locked herself in her baby's room. Brice knocked on the door but realized that he had to do what he had to do. He told her that he was about to leave, but she didn't answer him.)

Brice. I'm really sorry.

Michelle. You're damn right you're sorry. Just sorry. Now get out of my house!

(Brice couldn't believe how hurt she was. He felt terrible for what he had done to her. He headed to the front door, and slowly turned the knob, and spoke out loud.)

Brice. I'll be back, I promise!

(Once on the road, Brice couldn't help but think about the way that he left Michelle hanging. He knew that something was very wrong with it, but he was convinced that he did what was right. Soon as he got back in town, he immediately went over to Trisha's place, only to find out that she never went to the doctor. Trisha came to door and welcomed him with such wide and open arms.)

Trisha. Hey, sweetie. I'm so happy that you're back. We missed you so very much.

Brice. I wasn't gone long enough to be missed.

Trisha. Yes, you were, baby. I can't stand being away from you for even a minute. You know I love you, you are my baby daddy. And soon to be more.

Brice. Oh yeah. Wait a minute. What do you mean, and soon to be more?

Trisha. Just wishful thinking, honey.

Brice. Okay. Wait, I thought you said you were having complications. Shouldn't you be at the hospital or something?

Trisha. Oh. I meant to tell you. I'm much better now. It was just some bad leftovers.

Brice. You have got to be kidding me. You had me come back early for nothing. Damn it to hell, Trisha!

Trisha. Don't be upset, baby. You didn't come back for nothing. I'm here with your baby. Didn't you miss us even a little bit? And the kids are always asking about you. You do miss them, right?

Brice. Of course I do, but you...

It Feels Good, And It Feels Right

Trisha. No buts, sweetie. I don't want you to get all worked up. Maybe you should just go and lie down since you just got back in town. We have a lot to talk about so go get some rest.

Brice. There's more? I guess I should go lie down then.

Trisha. The kids are at my mama's house, so just go and rest your nerves for a while. And later I will have a surprise for you. Brice. Okay then.

(Brice went to take a nap in her bedroom, and when he awoke, Trisha was next to him in a black nightgown.)

Trisha. So how was it?

Brice. How was what?

Trisha. You know what. Your trip. And I know she gave you some. How can she resist? And I know she didn't ask you to come way up there for nothing.

Brice. Why are you so concerned about my trip? You obviously didn't want me there in the first place.

Trisha. Because I knew it was a mistake. It's not good to go backwards, you know. And I guess I was right. Besides, your future is right here. And I know she can't give it to you like I can.

Brice. Oh yeah? Why don't you show me better then?

(Trisha began to kiss on Brice and took off his pants. Once again, she gave it to him just the way he liked it. And they continued to make love for a while, but suddenly Brice realized something.)

Brice. Didn't you tell me that you were bleeding?

Trisha. Yeah, I was a little, but my mama told me that it's common in the early stage of a pregnancy. I'm fine now anyway. Don't worry, baby. Everything is fine. Also, we can have sex as much as we want to. And I know you like that.

Brice. I do, but we have to be careful.

Trisha. Be careful for what? I'm already pregnant, and I have two babies already, and they turned out fine. Besides, you and I haven't done anything that I'm not used to.

Brice. What?

Trisha. What I mean is that I didn't have any problems with my pregnancies in the past. See, that's why I love you so much. You are so caring and concerned. Now, baby, since you are back early, why don't we take the kids out to a movie or something?

Brice. All right. Let me go and get cleaned up first.

Trisha. Okay, baby.

(Brice went into the bathroom to take a shower. As he stepped in, he noticed a condom wrapper in the trash basket.)

Brice. What the hell is this, Trisha?

Trisha. What? (He showed her the basket.)

Brice. This, damn it!

Trisha. It looks like a condom wrapper, but not mine. I don't use them now, remember? And the last time I did was with you, and this isn't our brand.

Brice. Well, it's in your trash basket in your bathroom. To hell with this, and you...

(Brice went to put his clothes back on.)

Trisha. Wait a minute, baby. Don't go. It must be for my sister. She has my extra key. And sometimes she comes over when I'm at work. Let me call her.

Brice. You expect me to believe that?

Trisha. It's the truth, baby. You want me to call her.

Brice. I don't care what you do. I'm out.

Trisha. Don't leave, baby! I swear that it isn't mine. Why would I want you back so badly if I was messing around with someone else? I don't want nobody but you. I love you.

Brice. I can't tell right now. Something just doesn't feel right about this whole situation. I got to go.

Trisha. Please don't go. I promise I will get my key back from her and let her know, that she was wrong for that. I promise!

Brice. That's on you, but I got to go and think about this one. Tell the kids I said hello.

(Trisha grabbed her stomach and moaned.)

Trisha. My stomach is hurting, baby.

Brice. What is it? Some bad lunch meat from earlier.

Trisha. No, my mama said that stress could cause problems for the baby. You don't want that, do you?

It Feels Good, And It Feels Right

(Brice had compassion for her, so he tried to comfort her.)

Brice. Come here and sit down. Maybe we should call someone.

Trisha. No. I just need to relax, that's all. It will go away soon.

Brice. Are you sure about that? You look like you're in some serious pain. I'm sorry if I made this happen, but I just have so much on my mind right now. I know that you really care for me. And I shouldn't have a reason to be paranoid, but I'm a just a bit on edge right now. I've never been a father before, and this is all new to me.

Trisha. I know, baby, but it will be okay. Besides, you are a natural already.

Brice. I am, ain't I? I guess it must be meant for me to be a father then.

Trisha. Not just that. It is meant for you to have a family. I can't see you being away from your child. It just wouldn't be right.

(Trisha took Brice by the hand and looked him in the eyes.)

Trisha. Baby, don't you want to have a family of your own? You seem like a family man.

Brice. Of course I do, but I don't want to rush it, that's all.

Trisha. It's a little late for that, don't you think? Baby, you're about to be a daddy soon. Don't you want your child to have a stable family in a stable environment? And to be raised right?

Brice. Yeah, I do, because I didn't have that growing up.

Trisha. See, It's only right to be with me and the kids. This way, we can all be together as one complete and happy family. Besides, I don't want to have another baby and not be married.

Brice. Married! I don't know if I'm ready for that yet. I want to be really in love before I take that step.

Trisha. Baby, I love you enough for the both of us. And my kids love you so much also. It would be great. I know it, and I know you will learn to love me just as much as I love you.

Brice. I have to think about this. I have so much on my mind right now.

Trisha. Okay. Well, I'm never going to give up on us, just so you know, because I already know what's going to happen.

Brice. Really? Well, I don't, so why don't you tell me what you see.

(This was Trisha's big chance to really try to get Brice to see what she wanted him to see. After all, there was a wedding being planned behind his back.)

Trisha. I see you and I in front of our Pastor, saying our vows to each other. Me in a beautiful cream dress, and you in a black-and-cream tuxedo, looking so handsome. Everyone at the church is smiling because of how happy we are.

Brice. Really? I don't know about that.

Trisha. Well, that's what I see, and I didn't make this up.

Brice. Isn't the Pastor very strict about marrying people? I've seen the way he reacts to people who wants to get married. He will see straight through me.

Trisha. You'd be surprised, sweetheart. Pastor knows how much I love you, and I know he will not have a problem doing it.

Brice. Well, that's you. Not me. Besides, I don't need to be talking about this right now. Are you okay? Because I really need to go. Maybe you should call your mom and get the kids to keep you company tonight. I've had all I can deal with for today.

Trisha, but, baby, I was hoping that we could have a family night with the kids. You know they miss you, and would love to spend time with you.

Brice. I know, and so would I. Just not tonight. Don't you have to go to your mom's tonight for dinner?

Trisha. Yeah! But I thought that we could all do that, then take the kids to a movie. They didn't get many gifts this year, but they will love the ones that you gave them. Baby, thank you for always being there for them.

Brice. You're welcome! But right now, I think that I just want to go home and rest my nerves for a while.

(What Brice really wanted, was to go get a strong drink so he could get some things off his mind.)

Brice. Don't tell anyone I'm back just yet, okay? I'm sorry, but I'm going to leave for a while.

Trisha. Baby, are you serious?

Brice. Yeah, I'm very serious. Just go by your mama's house, and I will get with you later.

Chapter 3

It's time for a decision

(That was the first time in a long time that Brice left Trisha hanging. She was convinced that he would fall for what she was planning. She knew now that it wouldn't be as easy as she thought it would be. Brice left out, and as soon as he got around the corner, he called his friend Mario.)

Mario. What's up, bro?

Brice. What's popping tonight?

Mario. Man, I thought you were still out of town.

Brice. Yeah, I was, but my lady was tripping. You know how that is.

Mario. Nah, I don't know nothing about that bro, but you're whipped like that.

Brice. It's not like that, man. She was saying that she was having stomach pains from being pregnant.

Mario. Word! You are about to be a pappy. That's trippy, bro. You think she made it up to get you to come back?

Brice. Probably so, but it doesn't matter. What are you getting into tonight?

Mario. The spot where we used to go to is having a party tonight.

Brice. Cool. I need to unwind for real. You want to roll with me?

Mario. Nah, bro, but I'll meet you up there. I got to do something first. Hey! I heard that your ex has been going up there a lot. You might run into her.

Brice. Who are you talking about?

Mario. You know who! The one that had you whipped. That's who.

Brice. You say every female I meet get me whipped.

Mario. Cause they do, but Katrina, the one that had you so gone that you didn't even know that she had another man on the side for a good while.

Brice. Damn it! I don't need to see her. She is still mad at me for making her think that I got with her daughter. She even threatened to kill me. You know she's crazy.

Mario. You are the one crazy for making her believe that. Did you?

Brice. Did I what?

Mario. Get with her daughter, fool?

Brice. Nah, man. She's fine, but I would never do that.

Mario. She is nineteen, bro, so it's not like she's underage.

Brice. It just wouldn't feel right. She did try me a couple of times, but I didn't tell her mama. Anyway, her mama's the reason why she's so fast. She's probably been messing with older men too.

Mario. She is definitely fine! I saw her last night at the social club, looking just like her mama. I thought it was Katrina for a minute. Then I look over, and there her mama is. They are tight like vice grips, you know, but still she shouldn't be mad at you anyway. Her hot tail is the reason why her kids are a hot mess, but one thing is for sure. Brice. What's that?

Mario. She had you whipped. (Mario laughs)

Brice. Don't remind me. I was crazy about that girl. What was I thinking?

Mario. How fine she was every time you looked at her.

Brice. Yeah. She was fine. I remember the first time we went out. I met her at the steakhouse for dinner. Man, you should have seen her. When she walked in, everybody was staring at her like she was naked or something. She didn't even have anything sexy on. It's just the way her clothes fit on her. There was something about her that made me weak.

Mario. You mean her magical booty, or was it her milk chocolate skin with her pretty freckles?

Brice. It was something else, man, because I've had some fine girlfriends in my time. You know how I do.

Mario. Yep, and all of them get you whipped. (Mario laughs again.)

Brice. Not funny, but there was something about her for sure that put me in a trance. She could do whatever she wanted, and I didn't seem to care. She had me twisted for a good while, but I'm just glad that her spell wore off before it got worse.

Mario. I know that's right. Especially since she was messing with the biggest drug dealer around town. You better hope that she didn't tell him what you told her.

Brice. I'm not worried about that fool. I got people worse than him back at home.

Mario. Yeah, maybe you do, but they're back at home pimpin'. How's that going to help you here? It's probably for the best if you just stay away from her. She's like a rare disease that you don't want to be exposed to. You might want to go to the NCO club. I heard they are having a little something there also.

Brice. You going to roll with me, homeboy?

Mario. Not me. I'm going to the spot. They're going to have some of my shorties there. Some I can get with for sho. Ya heard me.

Brice. That's cold, bro. I thought you were my dog.

Mario. I am, but I'm not the one who got problems with hurricane Katrina.

Brice. I see how you are.

Mario. Like I said, not my problem. Holla at me when you're not scared. Peace.

(So now Brice was stuck on stupid, but not stupid enough to add fuel to the fire that was already lit. So he found himself back at home with a fifth of liquor and some black and milds,

It's Time For A Decision

that he picked up from the store. He might have dodged a bullet though, because if he would have ran into Katrina, it might have been a nightmare. After a while, he passed out but found himself being awaken in the middle of the night by a knock at his front door, but this wasn't the first time that he got a knock at his door in the middle of the night, but all the other times he just ignored them. Now the interesting thing was that he hadn't been drinking when they happened before, but strangely enough, he jumped up this time and stumbled to the front door.)

Brice. Who is it? Damn it.

(No one answered. Brice opened the door, and he saw a person walking away, dressed in what looked like a black suit.)

Brice. Who are you, and what do you want?

(The person didn't respond. Brice then ran behind the person and grabbed them by the arm. As the person turned around, all of a sudden Brice woke up, drenched in his own sweat. He rolled out of bed and ran to the bathroom. He felt sick and threw up. He then realized that liquor and nightmares don't mix well. After washing his face and composing himself he heard his phone beep. He had ten missed phone calls and several text messages from Trisha, but he wasn't in the mood to deal with her drama, so he turned his phone off. He then sat down and turned on the television. He began to flip through the channels to see if he could find something decent to watch, but all he seemed to find were infomercials and paid presentation programs, until he came across a church channel. Brice recognized the minister who was talking from a show that he had seen a while ago. So he decided to listen for a few minutes since he couldn't find anything else on that he found interesting. The minister was talking about marriage and how the union between husband and wife was supposed to be.)

Minister. The Bible says in Ephesians 5:22, "Wives submit to your own husbands, as to the Lord. For the husband is the head of the wife, as also Christ is the head of the church. And he is savior of the body." (Brice has a look as if he agrees.)

Brice. That's right.

Minister. So therefore just as the church is subject to Christ, so let the wives be to their husbands in everything, but husbands, love your wives just as Christ also loved the church and gave himself for her. (Brice has a look of frustration.)

Brice. What?

Minister. I don't know who this is for, but I'm feeling the Lord telling me that there is someone watching this broadcast right now who is contemplating marriage, but God is saying, 'Don't marry them.' If you do, then your anointing will diminish.

Brice. What does that mean?

Minister. It means that God's favor on your life will start to fade away because of your disobedience.

Brice. Huh.

Minister. That's right. God is saying that you are special to him, and he wants you to seek ye first the kingdom of God for guidance.

Brice. I sure hope whomever he is talking to, is listening. Dang, they sure are deep on this church channel.

(Brice turned the TV off and took some Tylenol, and then he went back to sleep. He woke up the next day and realized that he almost slept through Christmas. He felt bad about not spending time with

the kids, so he decided to call Trisha.)

Brice. Hello.

Trisha. Baby I've been trying to reach you all last night. Are you okay?

Brice. Yeah, I'm good. I just needed some time alone.

Trisha. Well, I understand, but I was trying to reach you because Ryan called, and he said he wanted to see the kids.

Brice. Who is Ryan?

Trisha. Their sorry excuse for a daddy. I told you about him when you and I first met.

Brice. Oh yeah, I remember. Why all of a sudden that fool want to see them now?

Trisha. I don't know.

It's Time For A Decision

Brice. What are you going to do?

Trisha. I don't know what to do, that is why I was calling you. I was hoping that you could help me make the right decision. After all, my kids do prefer you over him.

Brice. I don't know what to tell you. They are his kids, you know. I wouldn't want anybody to keep my kids from me.

Trisha. I never tried to keep my kids from him. He was the one who left us four years ago to go take care of somebody else's family.

He just left me hanging with no way to support my kids, and then I had to move in with my mama, and you know I hated to do that. And now after all this time, things are still not much better, and that deadbeat can't even keep a job. And it's hard to keep up with him for child support. If he doesn't have any child support to give me, then he isn't going to see them. That's how I see that.

Brice. You shouldn't do that. Maybe he has changed and want to do better. The only way for you to know is to let him see his kids. Maybe he will see the mistake that he made and learn from it. He can't make up for it, unfortunately, but at least he can learn from it.

Trisha. What do you mean he can't make up for it? Baby, he's gonna have to. I'm not letting him think that he can come into our lives after all this time and just act like nothing happened.

Brice, but it's okay. I'm going to do my part and make things right for all of us.

Trisha. Are you saying what I think you are saying, sweetie?

(Brice took a moment to reflect on what he just said, and he couldn't believe that those words came out of his mouth.)

Brice. Yeah, I believe I am, but let's talk about it later. Tell the kids that we are going to take them to the flying frog today. I want to see them enjoy themselves, and then you and I can talk about everything. I will be over there around three.

Trisha. Baby, I am so happy right now. You just don't know. I knew you would make the right decision. I promise, you won't regret it, baby.

Brice. Let's just wait until later, and we can talk about it. Okay?

Trisha. Okay, baby. I love you.

(They hang up, and soon as they do, Trisha immediately called everyone that she could think of and told them about Brice and her getting married. Starting with her mama.)

Trisha. Yeah, Mama, he's coming over tonight so we can set a date.

I told you he was gonna be mine. I knew it.

(On his way to see Trisha and the kids, Brice got a call from his sister, Dana, who he hadn't talked to in almost a year.)

Brice. Hello.

Dana. Hey there, little brother. I was thinking about you. Are you all right?

Brice. Yeah, I'm all right. Just surprised to hear from you, that's all. Is everything fine on your end?

Dana. Same ole same ole here. Everybody is fine. You were just on my mind.

Brice. Really?

Dana. Actually, you've been on my mind a lot recently.

Brice. Why haven't you been calling me?

Dana. I don't know. I'm sorry that I just decided to call, but it wasn't until I had this bad feeling that I felt like I really had to.

Brice. What bad feeling?

Dana. I don't know what is going on with you, but I feel like you are in danger. I know it sounds crazy, but I really feel like something bad is going to happen. Have you gotten into trouble lately?

Brice. Of course not! I don't get into any trouble. Why are you calling me with this? I thought this conversation would be about something else. The only danger or trouble I've been in is trying to deal with this dysfunctional family of mine. I'm glad that you called. I'm really tired of trying to make things right with my family and nothing happens. So starting today, my troubles are over. Okay, sister? I got to go. I'm actually on my way to start a new family with those who truly loves me.

Dana. Wait a minute. What do you mean?

It's Time For A Decision

Brice. I'm going to get married, and I don't care what anyone has to say about it. Bye-bye.

Dana. Wait, little brother, don't hang up. Brice, wait!

(Brice hung up on her and turned his phone off. Dana called back but continued to get his voicemail. She finally decided to just leave a message for him.

Dana. Little brother, I know that you are angry right now and hurting, but you're not the only one dealing with this drama. You need to think about what you're doing. I have been having dreams about you and your death. I didn't know how to tell you, but I feel like something terrible is going to happen. Please, please, forgive me for not calling sooner. Please call me. I love you (Apparently, there were issues between Brice and his family that hadn't been resolved. And to Brice, it didn't seem like they ever would be. Brice arrived at Trisha's place, and everyone was ready for their family outing. The kids rushed Brice and asked him where they were going.)

Brice. Ask your mom.

Kira. Mama, where are we going?

Dre. Yeah.

Trisha. I told you already. It's a surprise.

Dre. Well, I hope it isn't the flying frog.

Brice. Why is that little man? I thought you liked that place.

Dre. I used to, I'm a big kid now! That place is for babies like her.

(Dre pointed to his sister Kira.)

Kira. So? (Kira stuck her tongue out at her brother.)

Trisha. We know that you're a big kid now, sweetheart, but it is still fun there, right?

Dre. I guess so. If you're a baby.

Trisha. Well, it's a good thing we're not taking you there, huh?

(Brice looked at Trisha with an amazed look, then he mumbled to her.)

Brice. Where are we going then?

(Trisha mumbled back.)

Trisha. I don't know. Just find a place. (Dre noticed them whispering.)

Dre. Why are you whispering, Mama?

Trisha. That's grown folks' business, honey. You may be a big kid now, but you're not grown yet. So just sit back and mind your business, okay?

(Dre sat back and smiled at her.)

Dre. Well, I hope we are going to the house of pizza. Now that's where the big kids go.

Kira. I want Chuck E. Cheese's. Big kids go there too.

Dre. No, they don't. That is for babies too. You little baby.

Kira. Na-ah. You liked it when Mr. Troy took us there.

Dre. Shut up, girl. You don't know what you're talking about!

Trisha. Hush up, you two.

Brice. Mr. Troy. Who is that?

Trisha. Nobody, baby. Just an old friend, that's all. Way before you.

(Dre and Kira looked at each other with a surprised look on their faces.) Dre. Sorry, Mama.

Kira. Yeah, sorry.

Brice. Sorry for what? You said he was before me.

Trisha. He was. Not even important enough to talk about. It's okay, babies.

Brice. Yeah, it's okay, kids. That was in the past. (Brice mumbled to Trisha again.) There better not be any more surprises, I know that. Or else I'm gonna be in your past also.

(Trisha had this puzzled look on her face but didn't say anything. Finally, after driving for about twenty minutes, they pulled up to Dave and Busters. The kids were very excited. All of them were surprised to be there. Even Brice.) Trisha. So what made you come here?

Brice. I don't know. I saw the sign and just turned in. It just seemed right, I guess. Besides, the kids seem to like it.

Trisha. Yeah, they do, don't they?

Brice. Okay, let's go in. I'm looking forward to our family time.

(They went inside to get a table, and the kids asked for tokens so they could go play some games. Brice got the tokens for them, then told them to be sure to come back in time to eat.)

Trisha. Baby, I'm going to the ladies room, okay?

Brice. Okay, honey! I will be waiting.

(Trisha couldn't help but think that Brice was being sarcastic. So she had to somehow get his mind off the past. At the same time, Brice was thinking to himself that he wanted to find out if there was anything else that he needed to know about her past. So he got pretty anxious. Soon as Trisha got into the ladies' room, she called her mom.)

Trisha. Mama, the kids brought up Troy in front of Brice. What do I do?

Mama. How did that happen?

Trisha. The kids were talking about when he took us out to eat. Big-mouthed kids Mama, but that's not important. We are supposed to be having a special time tonight. I think he wanted to talk about getting married, but now, I'm not sure if he will go through with it.

Mama. Baby, if a man wants to marry a woman, he doesn't have second thoughts because of something so petty. If he really had time to think it through and is serious about marrying you, then he will still ask you. The last thing that you need is a man who can't make up his mind.

Trisha, but I love him Mama, I don't want anything to come between us.

Mama. I'm not saying that anything will, baby, but it's up to you to make sure that doesn't happen. If you love him like you say, then you need to do what you got to do to make sure you don't lose him. You understand?

Trisha. Yes, I do.

(Too bad, Trisha didn't have anybody else to talk to about relationship issues. Her mom wasn't quite the expert. However, she knew how to get by. She had been married twice before, and was currently separated with her second husband.)

Trisha. Thanks, Mama.

(Trisha composed herself and gathered her thoughts together. Then she left the ladies' room. As she was leaving, she ran into an ex-boyfriend, by the name of Mike. They had dated for about a year until Mike decided to leave her for a younger woman without kids.) Mike. Trisha, is that you? You are looking good.

Trisha. What are you doing here?

Mike. Actually, I'm here with my fiancée.

Trisha. Oh, really! So am I, and he has no kids. (Mike had a few kids that he neglected to tell Trisha about until late in their relationship.) Anyway, where are your kids?

Mike. With their mom. We're with her kids.

Trisha. What? I thought you didn't like to date women with kids? It seemed to be a problem when we were together.

Mike. I know, but I've grown since then, and now I'm open to new things.

Trisha. It was two years ago, Michael!

Mike. I know, but things are different now. I've finally found someone that is just right for me. You know? (Somehow Trisha found that hard to believe. Apparently, when she and Mike were dating, he seemed to distance himself from her kids. She later realized that he didn't want to be close to them because he didn't want a committed relationship with her.)

Trisha. You know what, Mike? I'm happy for you. I truly hope it works out for the two of you.

Mike. Thank you, Trisha. You really mean that?

Trisha. Not really, I hope you die, sucker. My new man is waiting on me, so you can kick rocks.

(Mike was left there, stuck with nothing to say. Then suddenly he spoke.)

Mike. Same ole Trisha I see. You're gonna drive that man insane.

(As Trisha walked away, she felt a heavy weight lifted off her. She always wanted to tell Mike how she felt about the way he did her and her kids. It was a good thing that she

It's Time For A Decision

walked off when she did, because Brice was headed toward the restroom.)

Brice. Is everything okay? I thought that you fell in the toilet or something.

Trisha. I'm okay. I was a little nauseous as I got up earlier. That's all, but I'm good now.

Brice. Are you sure? Because we can leave if you want to.

Trisha. No, I'm okay, really. I just need to eat something. I heard that not eating regularly can also cause issues when you're pregnant.

Brice. Okay then, but I got to say, for somebody with two kids already, you sure seem to know very little about being pregnant. (Brice was known for always being a straightforward person, but this time, he wished that he would have kept his mouth shut, because he could tell that he hurt her feelings.) I'm sorry. I didn't mean it like that. I'm just concerned, and I think that you should take better care of yourself. That's what I meant to say. As a matter of fact, have a seat. (Trisha sat down.) I was thinking that we should go to the pastor and tell him we need counseling.

Trisha. Counseling for what?

Brice. To see if we are ready.

Trisha. Ready for what?

(Brice made Trisha a little disappointed since he wasn't doing such a good job at asking her the way that she wanted him to.)

Brice. You know, getting married.

Trisha. Is this a proposal? If it is, then this isn't a good one.

Brice. I guess it is. You see, I've never done this before. So you will have to bear with me. Besides, you already said that you wanted to.

Trisha. I know baby, but there is a certain kind of way that I expected it to happen.

Brice. I tell you what. I will make this right. The way that I know to do it right is to first ask your parents for their approval. Then I will make my move on you and make it special like you want it. Okay!

Trisha. Your move on me? That's cute.

Brice. Yeah. I will ask your mom and dad if they are cool with it, then if they are, I will set up something special for you with everyone there to see.

Trisha. For real? You will do that for me?

Brice. Cross my heart I will!

Trisha. And hope to die?

Brice. I don't hope to die until my time is up. And only God knows that, but I do promise to do it.

Trisha. Okay. When are you planning on doing this?

Brice. Soon as we can get them together. I would actually like to see their reaction when they are in the same place at the same time.

Trisha. All righty then. I will see if I can arrange that.

(They began to eat, and the kids, in the meantime, were coming back and forth to the table while enjoying themselves.)

Kira. You're the best dad, Mr. Brice. No one has ever treated us as good as you. I hope you never leave us.

(Brice had this look of surprise, yet he felt so much joy inside from hearing her say that.)

Brice. Thank you, princess. It's my pleasure to keep that big smile on your face. Now let me see it.

(Kira gave him a big smile then a big hug to go with it. It was very obvious that Kira loved Brice more than Dre did, but it didn't change the way Brice treated him. Brice cared for both of them the same.)

Trisha. Kids, are you having a good time tonight?

Kids. Yes, mam!

Trisha. Okay. Well, here are some more tokens. Go ahead and play some more. (The kids gladly took the tokens and ran out to play.) See, sweetie, the kids love you, and no one has ever made them feel the way that you do.

Brice. I see, so out of all the men you've dated, no one has taken them to Dave and Busters?

Trisha. That's not what I'm saying, baby. What I mean is, it isn't about what you do for them. It's about how you make them feel just being who you are. See, with you, the kids even act differently. You have that genuine spirit about you that the kids can spot a mile away. You're a loving and caring kind of man that sticks out from the rest. That's why we love you so much. I really do hope that you do what you said a little while ago.

Brice. I will! One thing that I am is a man of my word, trust me. So let's go and check on the kids.

Chapter 4

Playing games and stressed out

(So Brice and Trisha went out to join the kids. Brice noticed a Mortal Combat game and immediately went to play it. He was doing pretty well too. Apparently, he had played it before. Mike noticed Brice and Trisha together, so he went over to see if Brice wanted to play against him.)

Mike. I see that you're pretty good at this.

Brice. Yeah. I used to play it a lot.

Mike. I can tell. I have too. You mind if we play a friendly game against each other?

Brice. You sure you want to do that?

Mike. Sure I do. It's just for fun, right?

Brice. Okay. Good luck.

Mike. Cool.

Brice, but where I come from, the loser has to do push-ups.

Mike. Oh yeah? You must be ex-military. What branch?

Brice. Army ranger. First and seventy-fifth ranger battalion. Huah!

Mike. Ranger, huh? Okay, Ranger. How about the loser does fifty pushups?

Brice. Diamond pushups sounds good to me.

(Trisha saw the two of them at the game and went over to Brice's side.)

Trisha. Baby, you ready to go?

Playing Games And Stressed Out

(Trisha knew that Mike only wanted to start trouble, so she had to stop it before it happened.)

Brice. No, not right now. I'm just getting started. Once I beat this guy, then we can leave, okay?

(Mike looked at Trisha and smiled.)

Mike. Grab a Snickers, because it will be a while. Your boyfriend may be good, but I'm better. See I'm marine recon ranger, boy.

Brice. Really? Okay, jarhead, let's see what you're made of then.

(Both guys seemed to be pretty good at this game, but Mike was having the edge so far. It was 2 to 1, Mike's advantage, and they were

playing the best out of six games.) Brice. Get me some more tokens, baby.

Trisha. I'm ready to go. Don't you think that we should leave?

Brice. Not right now. I'm not letting no jarhead beat me at my game.

(Mike was enjoying beating Trisha's man. And Brice was desperate for a comeback. Trisha was trying to figure out what she could do to make things go Brice's way. She gave him the tokens and then grabbed him around his waist and whispered in his ear.)

Trisha. Baby, you know what I'm gonna give you if you beat this guy?

Brice. What's that, baby?

Trisha. Anything you want. Brice. Anything?

(Brice got excited, and it motivated him to try harder. He beat Mike that next game and tied it 2 to 2. Mike heard what she said and remembered how much he enjoyed being with Trisha too. She had that special effect on men. He had hoped that he had experienced much more with her but didn't get a chance to. It took him off his game, and Brice won the next game as well. So now it was 3 to 2. Mike could win the next game and take into a sudden death game, but Trisha wasn't having that. She had enough. So she reminded Brice again.)

Trisha. Don't forget what I said, baby. Anything you want.

Brice. Okay, baby. I got this.

Mike. I don't think so, ranger boy.

(Mike got physical by bumping into Brice to make him mess up.)

Brice. Hold up, jarhead. I see you're a sore loser. I'm gonna have to teach you a lesson.

(Trisha remembered how dirty Mike could be, so she got ready to help her man. Brice and Mike had one round each, and the last round would determine a win for Brice or a tie, which would take them to sudden death. Brice knocked Mike guy down with a sweep.)

Brice. Yeah! That's what I'm talking about. Okay, jarhead, get down and give me fifty.

Mike. I don't think so, ranger boy.

(Brice looked over to see where Trisha was. As he turned back, Mike threw a right punch at him, but before he could connect, Trisha hit him in the back of the head with a pizza pan. Brice gave him one in the gut and then hit him with a right hook to the chin and knocked

him out.)

Brice. Get the kids right now. It's time to go.

(They got the kids and stormed out there as fast as they could. On the ride back, they looked at each other and laughed at what just happened.)

Brice. How did you know that guy was going to try and hit me?

Trisha. I kept my eye on him. I didn't get a good vibe from him. And he didn't play fair. So I took precautions.

Brice. Precautions? I like that. I guess you got your man back, huh?

Trisha. Always, baby. You gonna have mine tonight, right?
Brice. For sho!

(Needless to say, Brice and Trisha hurried and put the kids to bed. And then they enjoyed the rest of the night together as planned. The night was a long one, so they didn't get up until noon. The kids burst into the room and asked their mom.)

Kids. What's for breakfast, Mama?

Playing Games And Stressed Out

Trisha. Ya'll know how to fix some cereal.

Dre, but we want something else, Mama.

Trisha. I don't think so, babies. Mama's still a little tired from last night.

(She looked over at Brice with a grin.) Brice. Don't worry about it. I'll take care of it.

(Brice went into the kitchen and took out some grits and eggs. He noticed a little orange juice, but not enough for all of them, so he made some Kool-Aid for the kids. He added some toast for him and Trisha. The kids were very excited because they weren't used to this at all. Brice went into the bedroom with some scrambled eggs, grits, toast, jelly, and the rest of the orange juice, and he surprised Trisha with breakfast in bed.)

Trisha. What is this?

Brice. This is for saving my face. And a sample of what you may get in the future when you become my wifey.

Trisha. Oh really? Well, I tell you what. I need this to happen like yesterday then.

Brice. Don't worry, baby. It will happen soon. Enjoy your breakfast.

Trisha. Where are you going, hon?

Brice. I'm gonna catch up with a few of my homies, and we're gonna play some ball. Got to keep my game up, you know.

Trisha. Okay, baby. Well, be careful anyway. Brice. Always, baby.

(Trisha didn't know, but what Brice really was going to do was look for an engagement ring. He figured a nice ring from a pawnshop would do just fine for now. Then later on he could get her a new one. After shopping around a little, he managed to find a nice 1-carat diamond ring that was pretty affordable, but before buying it, he couldn't help but notice this guy who looked like he was having a tough time. The guy was actually trying to sell a 2-carat diamond ring.)

Brice. Hold up a minute, my man. How much you trying to get for that?

From Counterfeit to Priceless

Guy. I just want $600 for it. I really don't want to look at it anymore.

(Brice asked the clerk if it was real, and the clerk said yes.)

Brice. What happened, bro?

Guy. My wife was cheating on me, and to make it worse, I caught her in the act.

Brice. I'm sorry to hear that, bro. You gonna be okay?

Guy. Yeah, I'm good. I took the ring off the dresser, beat the dude down, and almost strangled that tramp. I just came here to sell it because I don't need it anymore, and I definitely wasn't letting her keep it. I guess it's your lucky day. I'm not going to tell you what I paid for it. I already feel like an idiot.

Brice. I feel you. I guess it is my lucky day. Are you sure you want to get rid of it this fast?

Guy. Yeah, I'm serious. Man, do you want the ring or not?

Brice. Yeah, I want it.

Guy. Okay then. I tell you what, you seem like a standup guy. If you promise me one thing, I will give it to you for $400. All I really want is to start over.

Brice. What do you want me to do?

Guy. Just don't rush into getting married. It's a very hurtful feeling to find out that you made the worst mistake in your life all because you didn't do it for the right reasons. Lucky for me, I didn't have any kids with the tramp.

Brice. No problem, my man. I will definitely not do that.

(Brice bought the ring from the guy and walked out of there with a better ring and more money in his pocket. Even though Brice got a steal on buying the ring, he couldn't help but wonder if that guy would be okay. Also, he thought about the promise that he made to the guy. He knew that he wasn't really telling the truth when he told the guy that he wouldn't rush into getting married. In reality, that was exactly what he was doing. His justification for doing so was because of how much he loved the kids and the fact that Trisha really seemed like she loved him enough for the both of them. Brice was convinced that as long as that stayed the same, then everything would be just fine. He even thought that there might be a chance that he would eventually fall in love with Trisha. Now, on his way back to Trisha's place, Brice got a flat tire. He pulled over to the side of the road so that he could change it. In the meantime, there were two guys in a red SUV who noticed Brice changing the tire. They turned around, then pulled up behind him.)

Guy 1. You need any help, man?

Brice. Nah. I'm good, but thanks for asking.

(Guy 2 got out of the passenger side and walked up to Brice.)

Guy 2. You sure, homie? Cause it looks like your front tire is going flat too.

(Guy 2 took a knife and stuck it into the tire. Brice knew he was in for it now. As Brice got up to approach Guy 2, the first guy hit him in the head with a gun. A 9 mm to be exact. Brice went down to the ground, then both guys began to kick him. They then robbed him and left him for dead. As they left, Guy 2 yelled out.)

Guy 2. Fool, you don't know who you was messing with!

(The last thing Brice saw was them drive off, then he lost consciousness. Several hours later, he woke up in a hospital. His ribs were broken, and his head was cut. He was in a whole lot of pain. The doctor told him that he was very lucky that it wasn't worse.)

Brice. What happened?

Doctor. You were attacked by two men while you were on the side of the road, changing a flat tire. You don't remember anything?

Brice. Nah. Are you sure I was on the side of the road. That doesn't sound right to me.

Doctor. Yes, sir. A homeless man saw you being attacked and went to get help for you. It's a good thing too, cause if he hadn't, you may not have made it. You had a lot of internal bleeding that we had to stop.

Brice. Where is the homeless guy now?

Doctor. We don't know. The police have been searching the area where they found you, but it's like he just disappeared. Once the police got to you, they called the paramedics, and they brought you straight here. We didn't find any identification on you, but it looked as though you were robbed. Do you know who you are?

Brice. What do you mean? What kind of question is that? Of course I know who I am. Do you know who I am?

Doctor. Sorry, sir, but I do not. Should I know you?

Brice. It's cool. You must don't watch TV or something or read the paper.

Doctor. I actually do both, but I don't know who you are. What is your name, sir?

Brice. Tupac Shakur. Doc, I've been shot five times before, and those haters still couldn't kill me. This isn't nothing.

(The nurse overheard what he said and burst out laughing. And the doctor looked very puzzled.)

Doctor. Are you really, sir? Well, do you know what hospital you are at?

Brice. Not really. I don't remember where I was, but if it's nearby my house, then I'm at Oakland Memorial. What's your problem, Doc? Are you trying to play me or something?

Doctor. No, sir, but I do have to ask you these questions. It's just protocol. When someone has gotten hit as hard as you did, we have to make sure that there hasn't been any kind of memory loss.

(The doctor knew that he was not Tupac, but she didn't want to alarm him any more than he already was. So she told him to relax and that she would have to run some tests to make sure that he was okay.)

Brice. Nah, I'm all right. I don't need no more tests. I just need to get out of here before one of them haters try to catch me up

in here slipping. I'm about to regulate on some fools today. Where my clothes at?

(He tried to get out of bed, so the doctor called security and had him restrained. She knew that there was something completely wrong with this man. He tried to resist, so more security personnel had to come in. The doctor sedated him to be on the safe side, then confined him to his bed with some restraints. After she saw that he was resting, she went to call one of her colleagues at Veteran's Memorial Hospital who specialized in amnesia patients. She knew that they would be dealing with something much more serious than that.)

Dr. Washington. Hello.

Dr. Rivers. Henry, this is Jamie. I have a problem down here, and I need your expertise. I need you here ASAP.

Dr. Washington. Wow! Must be serious. Let me see if I can get someone to take over for me. Where are you?

Dr. Rivers. At the hospital. I'll be here all day.

Dr. Washington. Okay, I'll be there as soon as I can. Dr. Rivers. Please, Henry, this a whopper.

(In the meantime, Dr. Rivers had Brice under surveillance while they tried to figure out what was going on with him. She noticed some kind of fluid on his brain during a scan of his brain. It seemed very unusual to her since she didn't specialize in that area. From her experience, the brain didn't have the type of activity that she was seeing in this one. She sighed and hoped that she would either wake up from a bad dream or that someone from the cast of Punk'd would come out in a moment and give her some sort of relief. Unfortunately, that was not the case here. And she now knew that she would be a part of what was one of the rarest forms of amnesia or personality disorders that she had ever seen in her years of being a doctor. Dr. Rivers went back in to check on Brice and noticed that he was starting to come off of his meds that she gave him.) Dr. Rivers. Sir, how do you feel?

Brice. I'm fine. Where the hell am I? Excuse me, Doc, but I don't remember nothing. How did I get here?

Dr. Rivers. Sir, I told you earlier how you got here. You were attacked by two men, and a witness told the police about it. You had no identification, so we don't know who you are at the moment.

Brice. What do you mean you don't know who I am? Are you serious?

(The nurse that laughed earlier was coming in and heard him a second time. She didn't find it funny that he really

From Counterfeit to Priceless

thought that they should know who he was. This time, she was convinced that he either had some serious type of injury or was playing a joke on them.)

Nurse. Mister, what is your problem? Do you know who you are or not?

Brice. I know who I am, lil' mama. The question is, do you know who I am? Cause if not, it's cool. You can always find out later over dinner tonight. You and Big Poppa can get real acquainted tonight.

Nurse. Doctor, this man thinks that he is Notorious B.I.G. now. Good luck with this one. I've had all I can stand. I'm going to go get some air.

Dr. Rivers. Thank you, Nurse Jackson. I have a specialist coming down to help me out with this one.

Brice. Bye, Nurse Jackson. With your fine self. Doc, what are you talking about? What do I need a specialist for? I feel fine. And I know who I am. You do know who I am, right, Doc? The nurse was just playing, right?

Dr. Rivers. Sir, the nurse wasn't playing with you at all. And as strange as it seems, yes, I do watch BET, but unfortunately, sir, who you say you are is not correct. And I must let you know that hours ago, you told me that you were someone else. And the sad news is that both of the men that you said you are have been dead for over twenty years now.

Brice. Stop playing, Doc. Who put you up to this? Did Puff tell you to do this? If so, I'm gonna kill him! Where is he? (Brice tried to get up and noticed the restraints.)

Brice. What the hell is this? Tell Puff the joke is up. This isn't funny.

(Security came back in because Brice tried to get out of the restraints. He bit one of the guards as Dr. Rivers tried to sedate him again. And Brice seemed much stronger than before, so they called for more help. They finally managed to control him, so the doctor gave him another shot to calm him down. Dr. Rivers was really frustrated now. She went out to give Dr. Washington another call.)

Dr. Rivers. Hello, Henry. I really need you to get here soon. It's gotten worse. My patient that I'm trying to treat seems to be having not only a change of behavior, but he also is experiencing some type of multiple personality disorder as well.

Dr. Washington. Hold up. What are you saying, Jamie?

Dr. Rivers. I'm saying that he thinks he is someone else every time I go in to check on him. I know it sounds crazy.

Dr. Washington. Jamie, calm down. There has got to be a logical explanation for this. I'm about to catch a flight now, so I will be there in a couple of hours. Okay?

Dr. Rivers. Okay, but please hurry. Nothing about this seems logical at all. I haven't seen anything like this before.

Dr. Washington. Okay. I will be there as soon as I can. In the meantime, please just relax, but don't go smoke. See you soon.

Dr. Rivers. Okay. I will try.

(Apparently, the two of them went way back, so they knew quite a bit about each other. And Dr. Rivers had been a smoker for fifteen years, until her grandmother passed away from lung cancer. Dr. Washington was there for her along the way, and eventually, they had a romantic relationship on and off during their residency together at St. John's Memorial in New York. They later chose to date for a while since they both relocated to hospitals in Louisiana, but Dr. Washington became too busy with more studying and traveling abroad, which led him to becoming a specialist in his field of study and research for the causes of long-term amnesia. So they drifted apart, but they still kept in touch every once in a while. Dr. Rivers got into practicing and developing new medicines at West Chase Herrmann Hospital in New Orleans, and Dr. Washington became a specialist at the Veteran's Memorial in Shreveport.)

Chapter 5

You're marked and set up, now go

(So Dr. Rivers decided to go to the hospital gym and work out for a while, hoping to relieve some of the stress and frustration from earlier. On the way, she ran into a fellow colleague of hers.)

Dr. Rivers. Dr. McGee, I didn't know that you were here today. Isn't this your day off?

Dr. McGee. Dr. Rivers. Hi. Yes, it is my day off, but I needed a workout today. The gym at my apartment complex is closed due to repair or something. Also, I needed to see the director about something anyway.

Dr. Rivers. Oh, okay.

Dr. McGee. You know what, while I got you here, I want to ask you something.

(They both went into the gym. Dr. McGee closed the door behind them and whispered something to her.)

Dr. McGee. Jamie, I need to tell you something, but I need you to promise not to tell anyone.

Dr. Rivers. I'm having a bad day today, Chuck, and I don't need it to get any worse. (She sighed.)

Dr. Rivers, but you know what? Sure. I promise. It can't be worse than what I've already experienced today.

Dr. McGee. Some of the vials from the operation, you know what, have gone missing.

Dr. Rivers. What do you mean missing? That operation was a failure remember. Everything should have been destroyed and not to be kept for your own personal use.

Dr. McGee. I know, but it was just too much to bear. I couldn't let all of my hard work go to waste.

Dr. Rivers. It was a team effort, Chuck. Does anyone else know about this?

Dr. McGee. No. You are the only one I've told.

Dr. Rivers. Okay. Good. Cause this could really turn out bad.

Dr. McGee. It's already bad, Jamie. We only tested monkeys and rats, remember? I've got to find the person who took them before it gets worse.

Dr. Rivers. And how do you plan on finding them? They can be in the hands of anyone. Someone who knows you and what we were doing has to have them, but who?

Dr. McGee. I thought about that already, but I can't come up with anything. It's driving me crazy! I'm trying to locate everyone who was involved and find out if there might be any out of the ordinary behavior.

Dr. Rivers. You sure you want to do that? It could blow up in your face if the person that took them knows that you are onto them.

Dr. McGee. I know, but what else can I do? We are the only ones that know about the effects of the drug. Besides, if I do nothing, then this town could be facing a disaster.

Dr. Rivers. Not just this town. The world could be facing an epidemic if that drug gets out. I will do some thinking of my own. We have to get to the bottom of this. Keep me posted as well.

Dr. McGee. Jamie, please, if you see or hear anything out the ordinary, please let me know.

Dr. Rivers. You mean besides the patient who thinks he is a dead rapper? I will be sure to let you know. Anyway, good luck, Chuck. We're going to need it.

(Dr. McGee just nodded and left with a frustrated and desperate look on his face. Dr. Rivers took a deep breath and exhaled.)

From Counterfeit to Priceless

Dr. Rivers. Just when I thought it couldn't get any worse.

(She stretched then got on the treadmill for a while. She then noticed that she had a missed call. It was from the director. Her pager went off, and she saw that the director had been trying to reach her. So she quickly gathered herself together and went to see him. She knocked on his office door and noticed that Dr. McGee was with him. The director told her to come in. she walked in, and the director told her to have a seat.)

Dr. Rivers. Director, you wanted to see me?

(Director Kevin Baisey, a tall middle-aged man from New Hampshire, had been working in the operating room for ten years before going to the emergency room for another five years as a supervisor. He had just recently took over as the hospital director, and he was known for being a very cool and level-headed doctor throughout his career, but Dr. Rivers could tell that he was not anywhere in the vicinity of being cool at the moment.)

Director. Dr. Rivers, it has been brought to my attention that you have been experimenting on your patients with a terrible illegal drug that should have been destroyed two years ago. (Dr. Rivers stood back up and tried to talk.) And before you begin to explain, I want you to know that we have two empty vials with your fingerprints on them.

Agent 1. You also have the right to remain silent. And you do not have to tell us anything that could incriminate you.

Agent 2. And you have the right to an attorney, and since you can afford one, you might want to get a good one. As long as he isn't Jewish.

(Agent 1 laughed as he took Dr. Rivers hands and placed them in handcuffs. She tried to resist, but the agent had control of her.)

Dr. Rivers. Chuck, you good-for-nothing bastard! How could you stoop so low? You are not going to get away with this!

(As the agents took her away, Dr. McGee spoke to the director.)

Dr. McGee. She has gone mad. I told you. I'm sorry that I didn't come to you sooner, sir. I just didn't want to see her get hurt, but at the same time, I couldn't go on any longer knowing and not do anything.

Director. Don't you worry, Dr. McGee. I appreciate you coming forward with this. I want you to see to it that there are no more vials in this hospital. The last thing I need here is a lawsuit. I'm counting on you to help me fix this, or else I will personally make sure that you do hard time for this crime. After all, you did know what she was doing.

Dr. McGee. Don't worry, Director. I will take care of it. I feel partly responsible for what happened.

Director. You're damn right you're responsible! But if you do get a handle on this, I might be willing to look the other way.

(Dr. McGee left the office with a smirk on his face, because he knew that his plan was working. First thing on his agenda was to go and check on Dr. Rivers patients, including Brice, so he could proceed with his experiment. He called one of his men and told him to come to the hospital.)

Dr. McGee. Rex, I need you to come up here with some of the men. Everything is a go.

(Dr. McGee hung up and made his way to Dr. Rivers office. He began to look over her files to see what the symptoms were. He noticed that Dr. Rivers forgot to write them down. He frowned and tore the paper up.)

Dr. McGee. I guess I have to find out for myself then.

(His team shows up like federal agents, and they transport Brice back to the new operation location. It was a secluded spot not too far from the hospital. It looked sort of like an abandoned mental institution. They moved Brice to a big room with padded walls and took the restraints off of him. Then they went to observe from an outside room. Finally, after about an hour, Brice woke up with a terrible headache. All of a sudden, he remembered being attacked, so he started swinging into the air. Then he fell to the floor into a seizure and began to have convulsions.)

Dr. McGee. Get in there. And make sure that we don't lose this one!

(A few of the men went in to check on Brice, and saw him sweating heavily. They grabbed a hold of him and put him back into his bed. They gave him an IV to help with the lack of fluids and to make sure that he didn't dehydrate. Dr. McGee left one of them to keep watch. They kept Dr. Rivers on the other side of the building, in what seemed like a holding cell. The agents that took her were actually a couple of Dr. McGee's guys. Dr. McGee wanted to make the director believe that Dr. Rivers was going to prison for what happened. That way, Dr. McGee could continue his operation without interference. In the meantime, Dr. Rivers was trying to figure out how she could get away. She realized that this plan was carefully thought out by Dr. McGee, but still she thought that there must be some way to stop him. The door to her room opened, and Dr. McGee entered with two of his men. Dr. Rivers charged at him, but one of the men stopped her.)

Dr. Rivers. You low down and dirty bastard! How could you do this to me?

Dr. McGee. Wait a minute, Jamie. The only thing I did to you was give you a much-needed vacation. And don't worry about your job. I got that worked out for you.

Dr. Rivers. What do you mean, you arrogant psychopath?

Dr. McGee. Watch your mouth now! You keep that up, and I will make sure that the real feds get you. My boys are paying the director a visit, and once he gets a double dose of the drug, he won't be able to press any charges against you.

(Dr. Rivers looked at him with disgust.)

Dr. Rivers. You can't do that. Don't you know that will kill him?

Dr. McGee. That's the risk I'm willing to take. Besides, it hasn't killed anyone yet. You ought to know that.

Dr. Rivers. What do you mean? I've never given any of those animals double of the dose. And I don't know anything about what you've been doing with the drug.

Dr. McGee. Perhaps not, but nevertheless, you are still an accomplice. After all, your most recent patient—you know, the John Doe who thinks he's a dead rapper—you've already given him two doses of the drug. Although they were small doses, they seemed to have done quite a bit.

Dr. Rivers. I can't believe you would do such a thing. You set me up, and you risked that poor man's life.

Dr. McGee. Well, believe it, I am sick and tired of being a follower, Jamie. It is time to take a stand and be a part of a greater good.

Do something that can change the world.

Dr. Rivers. You are insane!

Dr. McGee. No, I'm not! But I will tell you who are. People like you who keep doing the same thing day in and day out and expect different results. That's what's insane. I am very sane, and I am thinking about the whole world.

Dr. Rivers. I could have killed that man, Chuck. You can't be playing with people's lives like that. You're not God! That man may have people out there looking for him soon. What then?

Dr. McGee. That's not my problem. Jamie, I need you to join me in making history. We could be responsible for changing the mind-set of millions of people all over the world.

(Dr. Rivers didn't quite understand what he meant, but she was glad that she hadn't documented any of her work.)

Dr. Rivers. Chuck, the experiment was a failure, remember? It was a failure then, and it will be a failure now. Give it up. Don't you remember what a disaster it was? The rats with the strongest doses tried to kill each other, and the monkeys attacked some of our teammates. And when the doses were not strong, they just didn't do anything. Not eat, not drink, not anything. They were like in a trance. And eventually, they all just died. Don't you remember any of that?

Dr. McGee. Of course I remember everything. I was there, you know, but with your help with giving the drug to your John Doe, I was able to find out that the average human can live with up to two doses at least. All that's left to do now is figure out just how much of a dose is needed to accomplish the goal. You do remember the goal, right?

Dr. Rivers. It's impossible, and I won't go along with this awful plan of yours either.

Dr. McGee. Really? We will see about that. Maybe you will change your mind after my guys pay a visit to your grandmother. Or should I have your dogs put to sleep permanently? Your choice.

Dr. Rivers. You wouldn't dare!

Dr. McGee. Jamie, you've seen what I've already dared to do, so don't be surprised, okay? You said it yourself that I'm insane. We can do this the easy way or the hard way. So what will it be?

(Dr. Rivers realized that she didn't have a choice now.)

Dr. Rivers. What do you need me for anyway? Couldn't you just do it yourself?

Dr. McGee. Good try, Jamie, but you are the expert when it comes to mixing and experimenting. Besides, I'm going to need you to visit the hospital from time to time so I can have everything that I need to keep the operation going.

Dr. Rivers. What about your patients? Don't you even care anymore?

Dr. McGee. I care a great deal, but I mostly deal with kids. I may be a little ruthless, but I'm not an animal, but on the other hand, I don't mind using patients like the one we have. He probably was a low-life anyway.

Dr. Rivers. I'm talking about the work at the hospital, Chuck. Don't you care about helping those kids that need you? There was a time when you actually had a heart. You even encouraged me to do more. And the parents of those kids trusted their kids' lives with you. I've seen the spark in your

eyes when you are around those kids too. How can you just walk away from that?

Dr. McGee. What are you trying to do? Get me to shed a tear or something? Not gonna happen. Of course I'm going to miss my work with the kids. It has been my lifelong dream to save lives, but nothing compares to what we can get people to do with the correct dose of this drug. We can get more people to use the majority of their brain. And we can and will have more lawyers, judges, and even astronauts. All humanity will be smarter, and we can build a better world to accommodate the new us.

Dr. Rivers, but innocent lives will be affected in the process. That's not a plan. That's inhumane!

Dr. McGee. Stop with the patronizing, Jamie. Nothing you can say or do will change my mind. Besides, only a few more lives will be affected with your help. Together, we can see to that. And I'm pretty sure that it won't take us that long to come up with the proper dosage per person, considering the incentive I've given you.

Dr. Rivers. What's the status of my patient?

Dr. McGee. The last time I saw him, he was having some kind of episode, but don't worry. He is okay. You will see him very soon—as soon as you agree to help me save the world. So what do you say?

Dr. Rivers. I guess I don't really have a choice, do I?

Dr. McGee. Sure you do. Not really, but I would rather look at it like we are partners, and we are starting our very own business. The only difference is that our product will sell itself. Let's go and check on your John Doe.

(They made their way to the other side of the building where Brice was being held. In the meantime, back at the hospital, Dr. Washington arrived to see about his good friend, Dr. Rivers. Instead he found her missing in action. Apparently, there had been others trying to reach her also. He called her cell phone but got no answer. He went to her office to see if there were any clues to where she might be. He then heard a page for her over the PA system, so he went to see if she showed up. Once he got there, he came across Nurse Jackson, the same nurse that was working when Brice first came in the hospital.)

Dr. Washington. Excuse me, Nurse, have you seen Dr. Rivers?

Nurse. I'm sorry, but who are you?

Dr. Washington. I'm Dr. Henry Washington, a good friend of hers from Shreveport.

Nurse. Oh, that Henry. Well, I haven't seen her for at least three hours. I keep paging her, but I get no response. This isn't like her. She practically lives here.

Dr. Washington. Thank you, Nurse.

(Dr. Washington was really concerned now. He left his number with the nurse and asked her to call him if she heard anything.)

Dr. Washington. If you happen to see her, please tell her to call me.

(He couldn't help but wonder if her being missing had anything to do with the patient that she told him about earlier.)

Dr. Washington. Nurse… Jackson, is it? Nurse Jackson, would you happen to know anything about a patient of hers that was experiencing some kind of memory loss?

Nurse. No, I'm not familiar with that one, but if you mean the John Doe that came in who thought he was some dead rapper, then you're too late. The feds came and took him already, something about national security. You think they might be questioning her?

Dr. Washington. Maybe so. Do you know where they took him?

Nurse. Sorry, but no, I don't.

Dr. Washington. Thank you.

(Dr. Washington decided to stick around the hospital for a while with hopes of a call from his good friend or maybe he would see her come in from a long day of being interrogated by the feds. It dawned on him that her superiors must know what was going on. So he made his way to find out where the director's office was. As he made his way around the first corridor, he noticed that a lot of people were scattered about, and the police had made their way inside. It looked like there had been some kind of incident. He heard one of the doctors saying that the director had had some kind of heart attack. The director was transported to the emergency room so that he could be stabilized. It turned out that Dr. McGee had already sent some of his men over to give the director a strong dose of the drug. On his way out, Dr. Washington noticed what looked like federal agents. He approached them and asked if they knew where Dr. Rivers was.) Agent 1. No, we do not know anything about Dr. Rivers.

Dr. Washington. Then why are you here? You are here about the new patient with the memory loss, right?

Agent 2. How do you know about that? That is confidential, and it doesn't concern you.

Dr. Washington. Hell yes it concerns me! Dr. Rivers is my friend, and she called first to tell me about what is going on. So I demand to see her.

Agent 1. Sir, this is a federal investigation, and if you keep this up, I will be forced to detain you.

Dr. Washington. All I want to know is if she is okay. Can you at least tell her that I am here and to give me a call when she can?

(The agents acted like they didn't hear him and headed out of the hospital. Dr. Washington wasn't convinced about anything, so he waited. Then he got in a taxi and followed the agents.) Dr. Washington. Don't stay too close to them, Driver!

Taxi Driver. No problem, but it will be extra if this is dangerous. We don't have hazardous duty insurance, you know.

Dr. Washington. Okay, okay. Just don't let them know that we're tailing them. And don't lose them either.

Taxi Driver. Whatever you say, mister, but it will be an extra $20.

(They continued to follow the men to the abandoned site and parked where they couldn't be seen. The first thought that Dr. Washington had was that maybe the government was using the place for a secret experiment, but it just all felt wrong to him.)

Taxi Driver. Are you CIA or something? Cause if you are and you have to put me to sleep or something, I want my extra now so I can put it in my secret stash. I can't afford to wake up later and everything I have is gone. You know what I am saying, Jack?

Dr. Washington. Relax, man. I'm not an agent, just a concerned friend, but I do need you to stay here for a while.

Taxi Driver. I charge $20 an hour with $20 upfront, so give it up. And if you're not back after a couple of hours, I will assume that the real agents got you.

Dr. Washington. Okay, okay. I will try to be out soon.

(Dr. Washington sneaked his way around the building to look for a way in, but everything was locked. He climbed up to a second story, and broke a window to get in. As he quietly made his way down the hallway, he noticed a room with people in it. They looked like patients, but they all looked as though they were in a comatose state. The next room had a man in it that just sat in a corner. Dr. Washington gestured for the man to keep silent, but then he noticed that the man didn't even notice that he was there, as if he were in a dreamland or something. Dr. Washington then heard some pounding a little further down. As he went down, another man at the door of his room tried to get at him. Fortunately, the door was very secure.)

Dr. Washington. What is this place? And what are these people doing here? (He asked himself. He then made his way downstairs and noticed that the security was terrible in this place. It was as if they didn't care about what happened to the patients. He continued to look around to see if he could locate Dr. Rivers. Dr. McGee and Dr. Rivers were actually in a room, observing Brice.)

Dr. Rivers. What's wrong with him?

Dr. McGee. He had a seizure earlier, so we had to sedate him.

Dr. Rivers. What did you give him?

Dr. McGee. Calm down. We just gave him a sedative.

Dr. Rivers. We have to be very careful with what we give him now. The side effects of the drug are very serious, and we don't know what will happen when we give him something else. With the wrong combination of drugs in his system, it could cause him to be less functional.

Dr. McGee. Really? I'm sure he will be just fine, Jamie. If he hasn't gotten worse yet, we should be close to finding the right dosage.

Dr. Rivers. Be that as it may, but if you want my help, then you will let me handle the administering of any type of drugs, since you sabotaged me in the first place.

Dr. McGee. Okay then. Have it your way.

(All of a sudden, Brice woke up again. This time, he was calm and seemed to have this peace about him.)

Brice. Son, why do you have me strapped down to this bed? I'm not going to hurt anybody. Besides, you look like you bench four hundred pounds. I know you're not scared of little old me.

(The guard went over to Brice.)

Guard. You're strapped down for your own good. And don't call me son!

Brice. Son, for my own good? You've got to be kidding me. (All of a sudden, something came over Brice.) Let me ask you something. Do you want to be rich? Are you tired of working for somebody else? Robbing Peter to pay Paul? Let me tell you something. If you and your family desire to be rich, then you have to feel rich.

(Dr. Rivers and Dr. McGee couldn't believe what they were hearing, but they were all ears.)

Brice. You see, young man, you have to imagine yourself in a swimming pool of money. Go ahead and close your eyes. It's okay. I'm not going anywhere.

(The guard closes his eyes.)

Brice. Can you see it? Money up to your armpits?

Guard. Yeah. I can see it. Lots and lots of money.

(Brice started to loosen the straps, and Dr. McGee noticed it. He tried to get the guard's attention, but it was too late. Brice got out of his bed and walked over to the guard.)

Brice. Open your eyes, son. Do you believe in God?

Guard. I never thought about it.

Brice. It's okay. Let me tell you. God doesn't want you to be in your situation, but you have to acknowledge him for who he is, and he will give you the desires of your heart. He doesn't want you to be poor, so we're going to pray this special prayer. Say "God, thank you for dying for me on Calvary. Thank you for shedding your precious blood and washing me white as snow."

Dr. McGee. Get in there, you morons. The last thing I need now is this.

Brice. Please save me, Lord, and help me to live an abundantly blessed life with a cup that runneth over. In the name of the Father, the Son, and the Holy Spirit. Amen. Be blessed, my son. (Brice laid hands on the man, and the man fell out. Then the other men came in the room and laid hands on Brice.)

Dr. Rivers. Stop! He didn't hurt anyone. He just tried to help this man. Let him go.

(The men loosened their grip for a moment.)

Brice. Why am I here?

Dr. Rivers. You have been experiencing a multiple personality disorder of some sort. Since you came into the hospital, it's been one thing after another, but you don't experience them for a very long time.

(Dr. McGee made his way to the room.)

Brice. That's Ludacris. The devil is a lie, and the truth isn't in you, young lady. I refuse to believe something like that.

Dr. McGee. Well, believe it, brother!

Dr. Rivers. Why did you ask that man if he wanted to be rich?

Isn't money the cause of evil?

Brice. No, honey. The love of money is the root of all evil. You must not let money control you. Instead, you must control it, but if you love God and delight yourself in him, then he will give you the desires of your heart. Are you a doctor? Of course you are. Let me ask you something. Did you become a doctor to be wealthy or to save lives?

Dr. Rivers. To help save lives.

Brice. Okay. And because you delighted yourself in the idea of becoming a doctor, now you are reaping the harvest, correct?

Dr. Rivers. I live a happy life, if that is what you're asking.

Brice. Well, would you be happy if you were poor?

Dr. Rivers. I guess not.

Brice. You know what we can do for the poor? The best thing that we can do for the poor is to not become one of them. Because it is harder to be poor than it is to be rich. Think about it.

(Dr. McGee sarcastically applauded.)

Dr. McGee. Bravo, bravo. Thank you for the lesson on prosperity, Reverend, but we must find out why you are behaving this way.

(Dr. McGee gestured to his guys to put Brice back into his restraints on the bed. As Brice tried to wrestle with them, he called on God.)

Brice. God, please grant me the serenity to accept the things that I cannot change, the courage to change the things I can, and the wisdom to know the difference. Lord, Lord, I promise you that if you get me out of this, I will forever praise you and preach your gospel all the days of my life. Brice began to have another seizure, and this time, it looked very serious.

Dr. McGee. What's wrong with him, Jamie? We didn't give him anything this time.

Dr. Rivers. I don't know! He appears to be going in cardiac arrest. (Brice suddenly stopped moving.) He isn't breathing! We need to hook him up to the ventilator.

(Dr. Rivers knew that this was taking a serious risk, but she didn't want to lose him, so she had no choice.)

Dr. McGee. What's the damage? Is this one going to be a loss? I can't take another. Especially since we were so close.

Dr. Rivers. I'm afraid so, Chuck. I guess a higher power wanted this one.

(Dr. Rivers led Dr. McGee to believe that Brice was a lost cause, but instead, he slipped into a coma, and she could tell by the readings on the machine he was hooked up to.)

Dr. McGee. Damn it! Damn it! Damn it!

(Dr. McGee stormed out of the room and began to knock things over. Meanwhile, the guard was in the corner of the room on his knees, thanking God for saving him. He got up, then walked over to Dr. Rivers.)

Guard. I don't know who that man was, but because of him, my life has changed. I'm out of here.

(The guard casually left the building to go and start a new life. Brice was taken upstairs to a room where other test patients were. Dr. Rivers shook her head.)

Dr. Rivers. What a waste. I didn't even get to ask him who he thought he was this time. Maybe God is trying to tell me something.

(Dr. McGee told Dr. Rivers to go back to the hospital to see if there were any potential prospects.)

Dr. McGee. I want you to go back and act like things are normal. And, Jamie, remember if you cross me, then it's bye-bye Grandma and a deep sleep for your little mutts.

(Dr. Rivers gave him an evil look and left out. Dr. McGee told one of his guys to escort her out and to stay near her just in case. In the meantime, Dr. Washington noticed Dr. Rivers leaving out, and he sneaked his way back around so he could follow her. He told the taxi driver to follow them.)

Dr. Washington. Looks like they are going back to the hospital.

Follow them.

Taxi Driver. My friend, it is good that you are back. I was about to be out like outie 5,000, as you Americans say. Whoa, man! You like you've seen a ghost or something.

Dr. Washington. Worse, but if I have anything to do with it, this place is going down.

Taxi Driver. Whatever you say, 007. Or is it Bond? James Bond. I just love American movies, but, why do they have so many different guys play the man? Who was your favorite Bond, my friend?

Dr. Washington. Who?

Taxi Driver. You know. 007. James Bond. The roughest, toughest, and smoothest secret agent man to ever live.

Dr. Washington. Oh, that Bond. I'm sorry. My mind was someplace else. I like the newest one. I believe his name is Daniel Craig.

Taxi Driver. He is okay, but I like Pierce Bossman my friend.

Dr. Washington. You mean Pierce Brosnan?

Taxi Driver. That's what I said.

Dr. Washington. No, you did not. You said Bossman.

Taxi Driver. That's right. He's the boss of all the 007s. If you don't know, then you better ask somebody. You heard.

Dr. Washington. Whatever. Just get me back to the hospital. (Dr. Washington whispered to himself.) I wish I was the Bossman.

I'd put you to sleep.)

(So they arrived back at the hospital after about twenty minutes.)

Taxi Driver. Good-bye, my friend, and good luck on your mission.

Dr. Washington. And good riddance. Good God! The mayor let all types of people come down here after hurricane Katrina. I wonder if a black man as president could really make a difference. I guess there's only one way to find out.

Chapter 6

Unexpected or expected help is good

(Dr. Washington went back in to see if Dr. Rivers had made it to her office. He noticed one of the fake agents that he spoke to earlier. So he went to hide and decided to call Dr. Rivers.)

Dr. Washington. Jamie, its Henry. I'm at the hospital, just down the hall from your office. I know about the guys that took you. And I know you're being watched. Act like you're talking to someone else so they don't get suspicious.

Dr. Rivers. Grandma, I'm fine. Just working like usual. How are you doing? That's great to hear. I'm sorry I can't join you at bingo, but I hope that you win. Yes, ma'am. You know me. All work and no play.

Dr. Washington. That's good. We need to talk, Jamie.

Dr. Rivers. I was thinking about you too, Grandma.

Dr. Washington. I know about the abandoned site where they took you. And I know what is in there.

Dr. Rivers. Really, Grandma? I miss you too, but how did you know?

Dr. Washington. I followed two of the agents after they wouldn't tell me where you were. I thought something didn't look right with them, so I followed them to the site and snuck in the place.

Dr. Rivers. Now, Granny, that wasn't safe. Besides, they are not real. Just imitators.

Unexpected Or Expected Help Is Good

Dr. Washington. I figured, but it doesn't matter. I'm going to get you out of this, Jamie. Is there any way that we can talk face to face?

Dr. Rivers. Sure, Granny. We can do that. Soon as I come and visit you. I'm not doing much besides working anyway. Okay. I'm getting a little nauseous. I better go. No. I think it's something that I ate from earlier. I need to go to the restroom, so I will talk to you later.

Dr. Washington. Meet me at the one near the cafeteria.

Dr. Rivers. Okay, Granny. I'll talk to you later. I love you too. Bye-bye. (She hung up and walked out of the office.)

Guard. Where are you going?

Dr. Rivers. To the restroom. I am feeling nauseous. Do you have to watch my every move? You know that I practically live here. I won't be going anywhere. Or is it Chuck who doesn't trust you? Maybe he has someone watching you to make sure that you're doing your job. Guard. Impossible.

(The guard didn't seem to be sure, but he told her to not take long.) Dr. Rivers. Thank you. I knew some of you guys weren't all that bad. (He seemed pleased with the compliment.) Guard. Okay. Well, I will be close by.

(She went into the ladies' room and looked around for Dr. Washington. He was in one of the stalls, waiting on her. She went into the stall and immediately hugged him tight.)

Dr. Rivers. I am so glad to see you, Henry. When did you get here?

Dr. Washington. A good while ago. That's not important. Are you okay? Did they try to hurt you?

Dr. Rivers. I'm fine. Henry, there is so much to tell you. I may be connected to a very serious crime.

Dr. Washington. What do you mean?

(They began to talk for a while, but meanwhile back at the site, something very unusual was happening with Brice. Although, he was in what seemed like a comatose state, it would be better to say that he was simply in a deep sleep. While he was sleeping, he began to dream. In his dream, he woke up to the voice of an angel. "Arise, Brice! For you are about to do what thus says the Lord God." He awoke in this big king-size bed in a huge bedroom. It was very well decorated with vaulted ceilings, carpet all around, and a balcony that looked out at a lot of land. There were three cars in a circled driveway and a recreational vehicle, as well as three SUVs. The house had six bedrooms and three baths and was mostly made of brick. It was a two-story, fit for a king with all of the trimmings. As Brice attempted to turn over, an arm went over his chest. He saw a beautiful face with gorgeous brown eyes, long silky, wavy hair, and flawless chocolate skin. She then smiled at him with her pearly white teeth.)

Wifey. How did my Pastor sleep last night?

(She kissed him on the lips.)

Brice. I slept beautifully. God is so good. And how did my gorgeous and sexy wifey sleep?

Wifey. The same. You excited about today?

Brice. Baby, I'm excited about every day. Waking up to you every day really excites me. It's enough to make me say "Uhh! Nananana!"

(She laughed with him.)

Brice. A lot of times, I don't want to get out of bed. You feel me?

Wifey. I feel you, all right, but as flattering as that sounds, I know that your day will be a very busy one. So I must submit and be a good girl for now.

(He smiled at her and kissed her on the forehead before he went to take a shower.)

Brice. Rain check then?

Wifey. Of course, my love.

(While in the shower, Brice began to sing unto the Lord.)

Brice. The time is drawing near, and the world is still the same. It won't be long before my king comes back, then he will reign, but till my savior comes, my eyes are on the hills. I'll do what thus says the Lord and continue to obey his will. Do you know him, do you know him? Do you know him, do you know him? Do you know him, do you know him? Do you know him? You need to know the Lord.

(After he got out of the shower, he brushed his teeth then he walked into his huge closet and picked out a three-piece silk black suit, a white silk dress shirt, and a purple tie and handkerchief to match. He slipped on some very exquisite black gator dress shoes, put on some gold cufflinks and a solid-gold Rolex. Then he headed out to the front door, where his wife greeted him with his coffee and some sugar to go with it.)

Wifey. I will see you later at the church, baby. (She grabbed his hand and looked him into his eyes.) Wifey. Let him use you.

(He looked back at her with a sparkle in his eyes.)

Brice. I always do. I love you, baby. Wifey. I love you more.

(He smiled at her and made his way to his Mercedes Benz GL450 SUV, with a license plate that reads BEREAL. He lived thirty minutes outside of town, so it didn't take him long to arrive at the church. As he pulled up to what looked like a football stadium, he took the time out to thank God for what he had given him. After all, the church was sitting on one hundred acres of land that included a hall for events and an auditorium that sat 2,500 people. Also, there was a gym and basketball court. And a day care and fun center for all the kids. There were seven buses and seven vans on the property and enough parking spaces for five thousand cars. Last but not least, there was the chapel area, where all the services were held. It was separated from the rest of the facility due to it being so sacred to him. The outside of the chapel was that of a classic castle look and made of stucco all the way around. There were two sets of stairs that were at the entrance of the building. There were also beautiful flowers of all sorts that surrounded the entire chapel, mostly white lilies. Brice went inside the chapel where he met up with his assistant Pastors, his Secretary, and all of his Deacons so that they could conduct a meeting about church services for the last month. Also, he wanted them to pray together because he wanted them to touch and agree that his live interview with Yolanda of the Yolanda Show will go according to God's will. The inside of the chapel was gorgeous. It sat about five thousand people, and the pulpit was in the center of the church, so all sides of the congregation could have access to the stage. There were also big projection screens for the upper rows. Brice felt very comfortable in his pulpit, so he sat up there while his staff sat humbly in the pews and looked up at him. Brice asked them to all pray before they get started. They bowed their heads, and he said a prayer. "Heavenly Father, my God in heaven, we come to you on one accord, thanking you for just being you and continuing to show up and show out in all of our lives. We thank you for waking us up, and we thank you for your anointing. Thank you, Father, for your many blessings. May we continue to humble ourselves and pray and seek your face all the days of our lives. Father God, we need your spirit to pour out into this place so that people will recognize that you truly do live in this place and inside our hearts. Thank you in advance for all that you will do. In Jesus name I pray. Amen.")

Brice. Everyone, when you get a chance, I ask that you pray individually later for the interview today.

(Afterwards, they began to talk about the order of business, which was to discuss how the last month of services were. Apparently, they have a meeting once a month so they could continue to analyze the growth of the church and what they could do to make it increase even more.)

Secretary. Pastor, if I may. Assistant Pastors and Deacons of the church, the numbers for the last year has been pretty steady up until last month. We have experienced much more of a turnout ever since Pastor came out with his latest book. Also, many more people have been saved, and we have more new members. Praise God! Pastor, at this rate, the church will have to be renovated, or a bigger church will have to be built.

Brice. Praise be to God! That's what I'm talking about, people of God. Increase. When God increases in your life, so does everything else that is good. Number one is spiritual growth above all else. Without it, we are hopeless. And I want you ministers to preach, teach, and dream about increase in the abundance. It's what we represent here in our ministry. We want the people of God to look for increase in the spiritual, mental, emotional, physical, and financial. Make sure it's in that order, because God works in order, and he doesn't lie. We did not come this far without obeying every word that God has given to us, so let's not start disobeying him now. I have been praying for the ministry to increase in a way that everyone will know that God is doing a new kind of thing right here. And God has showed me that not only are we going to increase, but people all over the world will know just how good God has been to us. He favors us in spite of our enemies.

(The meeting continued for a while, but in the meantime, another car entered on the property. The song "God Favors Me" was blasting away. In the car was Minister Ricky Martinez. He was the choir director. He was known for being a pretty happy-go-lucky kind of guy who loved God. Apparently, there was choir practice that day as well. The choir was going to be participating in a big gospel explosion later in the month, and Minister Ricky wanted to make sure that they were at their best. To some of the choir members, he could be pretty aggressive, and demanding, but no one complained because two of the members that worked with him signed with gospel recording labels. And as a token of gratitude, they made sure to give credit to Minister Ricky for pushing them to their true potential. Obviously, they blessed him with money, and cars, and other gifts, but none was more precious to him than his music equipment—new drums, keyboards, and state-of-the-art microphones and speakers, all which he loved to play with as often as he could. So when he wasn't working with the elderly at his nursing home job, he came to the auditorium with a few of the church musicians and choir members. As he went in to get ready for choir rehearsal, Brice was finishing up with his staff.)

Head Deacon. So, Pastor, are you going to be nervous about today?

Brice. Actually, I'm going to do like Paul did when the Lord told him not to worry about what to say, for the Holy Spirit will speak through you at the chosen time. So the answer to your question is no. I'm not going to be nervous at all. Excited, yes, but not nervous. I'm going to decrease as God increases.

(They all touched and agreed with Pastor, and one of the assistant Pastors prayed them out. The meeting was over, and everyone went to get ready for the interview. Initially, Yolanda had asked Brice if she could interview him in front of his congregation, but he declined because he felt like there would be a distraction, but later on, after he prayed about it and discussed it with his wife and his staff, he then decided to let the spirit move him, and he granted Yolanda her request, but he had warned her that depending on how the interview went, there might be breakthroughs, because of the anointing of the Holy Spirit that resided inside the chapel and, of course, the anointing that God particularly gave him. Yolanda was okay with it and actually welcomed it because it would only help her ratings at her show. And she was aware of the controversial remarks and statements from the critics and the media toward Brice and his ministry. There were some who did not like the radical teachings that he wrote about in his book, or what went on in his ministry. As Brice headed toward his office, he noticed some people coming in with cameras. Apparently, Yolanda had her team get there early so they could set up everything.) Brice. Hey, hey, you guys are pretty early.

Yolanda's assistant. Yes, sir. We are. So we can take a look at the place and get our equipment set up. Yolanda will not settle for less than perfect. So we don't give anything but that.

Brice. Okay. Just coordinate with Deacon Rogers, and he'll show you around.

Yolanda's assistant. Thank you.

(So Yolanda's team went with Deacon Rogers, and everyone else left out. Brice told his secretary that he would be in his office for a while and not to interrupt him unless it was his wife. He turned his cell phone off and went into his specially made prayer closet that he used before his regular church services and anytime that he really needed to hear from God. He lays down on his face and tells God that he really needed to hear from him.)

Brice. Father God, thank you for taking me to where I am today and for allowing me to long suffer for your sake. Today I come to you as humbly as I can, asking you to continue to show up and out in me. Not like you have been, but with an even greater anointing Lord, because I feel like the enemy is going to increase his camp and try to tear me down. I know that with you, Lord, that I can do all things, but if it be your will, please increase in me with a fresh, and mysterious anointing than only you can understand. If it had not been for you, Lord, little poor old me would not be here today. So I say, thank you for what you have done for me and for what you are about to do. I praise you, I honor you, I lift up your name, and I will forever love you, my God. Thank you, Father. In the name of the Father, the Son, and the Holy Spirit, Amen.

(Brice continued to lie on his face for a while in reverence to God. After a while, he lifted up his head and looked up. He smiled and thanked God again. He looked as if something had been revealed to him, cause now he had a look of a man who was totally confident and was in control, with authority. He left out of his office with assurance that everything would be just as God wanted it to be. As he headed back inside the chapel, Yolanda's assistant approached him.)

Yolanda's assistant. Sir, we are all set up and ready. Are you ready to get prepped?

Brice. Yes, I am ready, and please call me Brice.

Yolanda's assistant. Sir, I don't think that I can do that.

Brice. Well then, you can call me Be Real. I insist. 'Cause sir makes me feel old. And I'm not ready for that just yet.

Yolanda's assistant. Yes, sir. I mean… yes, Pastor Be Real. Okay. Let's get you to make up.

Chapter 7

Going from completion to a new beginning

Yolanda's assistant. We need to make sure that you look your best. Yolanda will be here shortly.

(In the meantime, a lot of the members and Yolanda's fans had showed up to the church. They began to enter the chapel. Since the service wasn't normal, it was a first-come-first-seat sort of speak. After an hour went by, the chapel was practically full to capacity, and right on time was Yolanda and the rest of her team.)

Yolanda. I'll be darn! So this is where it all takes place. Home of the demon chasers. I'm a little intimidated, and that doesn't happen to me.

Brice. Why is that, Yolanda?

Yolanda. I'm used to being the one they come to see. Right now, I don't know if they are here to see me or you.

Brice. How about we just say that they are here for a wonderful time.

Yolanda. Of course. We could say that. Okay. How are we looking?

Yolanda's assistant. We are ready to go Yolanda. Everything is set up, and the stage is ready just the way you wanted it. Yolanda. Good job, Sheila. Okay, let's get started! (Yolanda got her makeup and began to get prepped for the

Going From Completion To A New Beginning

interview as well. Then they headed to the stage so they could get comfortable.

A few minutes went by.)

Cameraman. You're on in five minutes, Yolanda. (Yolanda smiled and nodded.) Yolanda. Are you ready for this interview?

Brice. Yes, I am.

Yolanda. You know there is a lot of talk that your ministry is trying to separate itself from all of the rest of the world.

Brice. That is the plan, Yolanda. My father says that if his people who are called by his name will humble themselves and pray and seek his face and turn from their wicked ways, then he will hear from heaven. Then he will forgive them for their sins, and he will heal their land. He also says that we he will see them and listen to their prayers that they pray in this place, and it will become holy.

Yolanda. So the church will become holy?

Brice. Yes, but he also means our temple, which is our body, and he refers to himself being worshipped inside the temple forever in spirit and in truth.

Yolanda. Wait a minute! We need to get this on camera. Cameraman. One minute, Yolanda.

(A message appeared on the big screens and, by the signs, asking everyone to be quiet. Going live!)

Cameraman. Ten seconds. And 5, 4, 3, 2, and 1. We're live.

Yolanda. Hello, everyone, and thank you for once again joining me on the Yolanda Show. Today, I have on the show for a very special one-hour exclusive interview, a man who has been singled out by many American churches and its counterparts, because of his unusual and radical teachings in his latest book, Demon Chasers. He is also the author of the bestselling book Acts of Desperation, which I've read by the way. And it's incredible. He is also the founder and senior pastor of this great, big church Living Testimony Church, home of the Radical Praisers and the Demon chasers. Please welcome with me Pastor Brice Realton.

(The audience clapped, and most of them stood to their feet. The applause lasted for about a minute.)

Yolanda. Thank you for coming to the show, Pastor Realton.

Brice. You're very welcome, Yolanda. And thank you for having me.

Yolanda. You are very welcome as well. Before we get started, I want you to clear something up for me, if you don't mind.

Brice. Sure.

Yolanda. You were telling me something, before the show about God, and how he will be worshipped in the temple forever. For the folks here and at home, can you please explain what he meant? And by the way, I would like to thank all of you wonderful people in our audience for coming out today.

(Brice smiled and then proceeded.)

Brice. Well, Yolanda. I was simply referring to a scripture in the Old Testament part of the Bible, 2 Chronicles 7:14 through 16. It was during the reign of King Solomon, who was the richest and wisest king to ever live, but the scripture talks about God appearing to Solomon in a dream, telling him to use the temple that he builds for the Lord, as a place for sacrifices that are pleasing to God, but after a period of time, God will stop the rain from coming down and send locusts to destroy the land, and there will be sicknesses upon some of his people so that he can separate the righteous from the unrighteous. And in verses 14 through 16, he says, "If my people who are called by my name will humble themselves and pray and seek my face and turn from their wicked ways, then he will hear from heaven." Then he will forgive us for our sins and then heal our land. And then he will listen to our prayers prayed in this place. And it will become holy.

Yolanda. Okay! Does he mean in the church?

Brice. Yes, he does, but it goes deeper than that. You see, the church is a temple, but so is our body. Each one of us has a body created by God, and it was created in his image. So the church is supposed to be the body, which is each one of us. And once we accept Jesus as our Lord and Savior and se parate ourselves from the evil in this world, then God will choose our bodies to be a place of worship like the temple, but we must choose to worship him. He won't make us. We have to be willing and able to accept him.

Yolanda. Wow! That is very deep, indeed. Hold on to your seats, everyone. Because I believe there is much more where that came from. So, Pastor, how did you get involved in the church?

Brice. I actually didn't grow up in the church. I went to church a few times with my Aunt Delores when I was a teenager, but God had his hands on me since I was a baby. I didn't enjoy the baptism of the Holy Spirit until I was in my twenties.

Yolanda. Wow! And look at you now, a mega church with thousands of members. Who could have known that?

Brice. Only God, Yolanda. You see, I've been saved for fifteen years, but that doesn't have anything to do with my success in the Lord. God already knew what he wanted me to be doing before I did it. I just had to become humble and separate myself from evil, and the rest is history. You see, God's vision that he gave to me was plain. Not so simple that a caveman could do it, but it was plain to see for me.

Yolanda. If you don't mind me asking, what was the vision?

Brice. Have you ever heard of the phrase "Many are called, but few are chosen"?

Yolanda. Yes, I have.

Brice. There are a few like me who have been chosen by God to come out from among the rest and to humble themselves like they have never done before. Because the task that God has given us will require plenty of prayer, patience, praise, and preaching. I call them the five Ps. Of course, the last one is persecution. In my book, I talk about in detail just how the first four work together so we can deal with the persecution that comes from doing them. See, God knows that <u>persecution</u> is something that most of us are not equipped for, so we must first long suffer for patience, and we must have a powerful prayer life and remember to give God praise in our good times as well as our bad times. And last but not least, my favorite—to preach the gospel! Amen. And through Jesus Christ, we are strengthened and can do all things. Whether

From Counterfeit to Priceless

I am the first to come out or not, does not matter to me. There is a prophecy that must be fulfilled, and those who are chosen know who they are. I am empowering them through my book, and by doing this interview. I ask that they step out and join me in this fight!

Yolanda. And what fight is that?

Brice. Yolanda, we are in a spiritual warfare, and it's been going on since the beginning. And everyone has a choice to fight against good or evil.

Yolanda. So you are saying that even though many are called and few are chosen, everyone else still has to be a part of it?

Brice. Exactly! Remember that every one of us was created in God's image. No matter what the culture, race, or religion, we all come from the Creator. The best way to really understand is to get my book, but if you want to know where I did my research, then you can pick up the book by the greatest author that ever existed. It's in most bookstores and even some of your local grocery stores. Amen.

Yolanda. On that note, we will be right back to find out more from Pastor Realton and his church of Demon chasers. Stay tuned, everyone. We'll be right back.

Cameraman. And go to commercial.

Yolanda. That was very insightful, Pastor Realton. Do you think that maybe you can answer some of the controversial questions that some of the critics have been asking?

Brice. I'm prepared to answer any questions from anybody. Of course, that's if I have the answer.

Yolanda. Right. And could you be a little simpler in your answers? We have a lot of people who are here, and at home who may not get a clear understanding of what you are saying. I will try, Yolanda, but God is in control of my life, so I give it the way that he wants me to.

Yolanda. Thank you. I'm going to be asking you to share with us in a little more detail about your book, and to discuss some of the reactions of your critics. If you are okay with that.

Brice. I'd be more than happy to talk about it.

Cameraman. On in one minute.

Yolanda. Okay, great. And remember, answers that everyone can understand, even me. I want all the people to know the truth.

Brice. And the truth they shall get.

Cameraman. And 5, 4, 3, 2, 1, you're live!

Yolanda. Hello once again, and thank you for tuning in to the Yolanda Show. Today, I've been talking to Pastor Brice Realton, founder and senior pastor of Living Testimony Church and author of the new book Demon Chasers, which has been getting a lot of criticism from other Christians. Pastor Realton has come on the show to answer some of the questions regarding the controversy concerning his book and his ministry. Thank you once again for coming on the show.

Brice. My pleasure.

Yolanda. So let's begin. In your book, you talk about seeing demons as if they were regular people. How is that possible?

Brice. That is correct, Yolanda. When I was thirty, I attended church one Sunday. Service was normal, just like most times, but this particular Sunday, my pastor had a guest speaker from out of town. I had never seen the man before, but there was something different about him. I couldn't see it at first, but when he got up to preach, I noticed that he had what looked like a shadow follow him to the pulpit. Now, most of us would agree that a shadow doesn't appear unless there is sunlight, or at least a very bright light shining on us. And a shadow has to reflect off something solid and light colored, right? Well, to make sure that I wasn't delusional, I asked the person next to me if he saw it too. He said no and asked me to be quiet. I tried to compose myself and concentrate on the sermon, but as the man preached, the shadow rose up and appeared to me as a spirit of evil. It had two horns on its head, fiery eyes, and big sharp teeth that protruded out of its mouth. I could see it clear as I see you right now.

Yolanda. What did you do when you saw it?

Brice. I jumped up out of my seat and ran to the restroom. I washed my face and tried to calm down. I pinched myself because I thought that maybe it was a bad dream or something. After a while, I went back out there. I sat in the back of the church this time, because I was embarrassed for getting up like I did, but it didn't seem to matter, because the speaker came down to the congregation. He went away from his sermon about serving and started laying hands on people who wanted power, and wealth. I thought that was very odd to change up like that in the middle of a subject like serving. Also, I was pretty sure that the Bible said that there were three reasons why you should lay hands on people. Healing, deliverance, and receiving an anointing. The speaker went back up to the front and asked people to come up for a special prayer if they wanted this power and wealth. As the people went up, I noticed that they also had evil spirits following them like a shadow. After witnessing this, I went home, and prayed, and asked God to show me what it all meant. My father told me that he was giving me the gift to see what he wanted me to see so that I can fulfill the purpose that he had for me, which is to help separate the real from the fake. He said that we all have evil in us, because we were born into sin, but in order to be separated, we must be willing to be like Christ. I asked him how that is possible since Jesus Christ was not born into sin nor the seed of a man. God said, that we must be willing to have a Christ like death in order to truly be separated from the world.

Yolanda. Wow! I see the audience is in awe of this wonderful testimony, Pastor Realton. And I must say that I am as well. And I know you guys want more, right?

(The audience yelled out yes.)

Yolanda. Me too, but it'll have to be right after we come back from commercial. When we do come back, we're going to find out more about Pastor Realton's book Demon Chasers and the mission of his ministry. We'll be right back!

Cameraman. And go to commercial.

Yolanda. Wow again! I don't know what to say. That is such an amazing story. I really want to thank you for coming on my show and sharing with everyone what you and your ministry is about.

Brice. You're welcome, Yolanda, but I want you to remember something. God chose your show in order for me to make it known, and he knew just how things would turn out. One thing about God—he does things in order. And he is in control of my life, so I have to be in order as well.

Yolanda. Is he always in control?

Brice. Yes, he is, but he will let us make our own choices in life. He gives us free will. Why do you think that we get into predicaments sometime? God allows us to choose how we want to live our life. Meaning, we get to choose who we will serve. God or evil. I call it justification.

Yolanda. What do you mean?

Brice. God created us in his image, not to treat us like puppets, but to try and get us to freely choose to be like him and serve him. Only him. And when we decide to serve him, then his work, and who he is will be justified.

Yolanda. Interesting.

Cameraman. We're back on in 5, 4, 3, 2, and 1.

Yolanda. We're back with Pastor Brice Realton, author of the book Demon Chasers. We've been discussing some of the book and how the inspiration of writing it came about. So, Pastor Realton, you were saying that the mission of your ministry is to separate the real people from the fake ones. How can you really do that? I mean isn't that impossible to do without actually getting to know people first?

Brice. For most people, that is correct, but there are a few who were chosen by God for such a time as this. And now is the time for all of us to rise and show everyone who has ears to hear and eyes to see.

(Pastor Realton gets up and starts to preach to the people. And the spirit of God was starting to move in the church just like he told Yolanda it would.)

Brice. People of God, I am here on behalf of my father, the one and only most high God. And he says the time is now! Turn away from your wicked ways and seek first the kingdom of God before anything. Some critics want you to think that I am a fake and a fraud, but I say to you and to them, that if God be for me, then who can be against me. These same critics who say that I am not who I profess to be, will not fellowship with me or my ministry, because they are afraid that my father will reveal their true selves to me. You know who you are.

(Yolanda gestured to the cameraman to keep the camera on Pastor Realton. Apparently, she recognized the power of God in this place. She had hoped to ask him a few more questions, but somehow she felt that the answers were coming.)

Brice. So they want to know if I am a Demon chaser. Okay. Let's find out. (He stepped off the stage and went into the audience. He walked over to this young woman.) Young lady, do I know you? Lady. No, sir.

(The lady smiled and seemed to be happy about being the first to be approached.)

Brice. Then how do I know that you are cheating on your husband? (Her smile quickly changed to a frown. She didn't know what to say.)

Brice. Before you say anything, I want you to know that God will forgive you, and he wants to forgive your husband as well.

(Her husband was sitting next to her, and he was looking like he didn't know what was going on.)

Brice. That's right, young man. You too. God wants to forgive you both, but you must go to him and seek it. Those prostitutes that have been in and out of your house, are only the enemy's way of trying to tear your marriage apart.

(Brice looked at the wife.)

Brice. And that man, who comes to your house, when your husband leaves to go to work. He isn't what you really want.

(The audience was overwhelmed by what had just happened.)

Brice. I know, I know, you are all wondering why did this just happen. And you are thinking that a Pastor should not do what I just did. You are exactly right, but Pastors wouldn't be able to do this unless you have told them your business. I have never met these people, but God knows them both. He knows everything, and you can't hide anything from him. I know right now some of you are afraid and hoping that I don't come up to you next, but you can stop wondering if I am or not. I don't desire to do that, but God is in control, and he will reveal whatever dark secrets that some of you have in due time. Remember, everything that is done in the dark will always be revealed in the light, sooner or later. The best advice that I can give to those of you who I am referring to is to turn away from your wicked ways and to ask God to forgive you of your sins. Then seek him for guidance to a better life. He already knows your heart, and he will change your life forever. Just like he did mine. Amen.

(Pastor Realton turned back to the puzzled and very embarrassed couple.)

Brice. God knows your heart daughter. He knows your heart son. And he wants you both to accept him. And remember, God already sent his only begotten Son here to earth to die and save each and every one of us. So we are all saved, but there is a process before you can have your name written into the book of life, and you must willfully ask Jesus to come into your heart and become your Lord. Isn't that something? He comes to our rescue when most of us didn't even know we needed rescuing. Hallelujah! (Pastor Realton put a hand on each of them.)

Brice. Be gone, Satan!

(The couple both received the Holy Spirit, and immediately Pastor Realton could see the evil spirits fleeing as fast as they could. He then called some of his ministers over to pray for the couple. Then he gestured for a few other ministers to follow him as he walked up and down the aisles.)

Brice. For all of you, married couples, God wants you to honor your marriage. Be faithful to him first then to each other, and you will see yourselves prospering together.

(By this time, the place was filled with worship, and the spirit of God was moving all around the place.)

Brice. There is a good angel and an evil spirit that we all have to deal with on a daily basis. If it were not, so then we would be in total control of our own lives. People, the only control that we have is to make our own decisions. Once again, we must make a decision, and I encourage you to make the wise one. Ask yourself, "Do I want everlasting life in heaven, or do I want to live in hell for the rest of my life?" Either way you go, it will be forever. Where is up to you!

(He looked around the whole place.)

Brice. Where are my radical praisers at? I know you are in here. If you are willing to die a Christ-like death, I want you to come on down here. What I am about to do will require much help, so I need some people of God who loves him like I do.

(The chapel had thousands in it, but a few hundred came down and stood around the pulpit.)

Brice. Father God, I pray that you sharpen the hands of your people right now. Please give them the power of your spirit, so together we can go out and defeat the enemy. Let your anointing rest upon each one of us today. We are your soldiers in your army, Lord. Thank you, Father. Amen. Okay, soldiers for Christ, I want you to separate into sections, and I don't care about how you do it, but each person in here will experience the power of God today. And by the power of the Almighty God, there will be deliverance. Amen.

(So the people who came down, separated into sections, and they went up and down each aisle and rows laying hands on everyone.

There was shouting and praise everywhere. There weren't enough of ministers or ushers to handle the movement, but Pastor Realton told them not to worry about it.)

Brice. God is in control, and he will take care of his people. He loves you, and right now, the devil has got to go.

(He approaches those who have demons in them, but as he touched them, the demons fled away. He passed by people speaking, get out, get out.)

Brice. Get out of my brothers and sisters. You don't belong here.

Going From Completion To A New Beginning

(Even some of those who didn't get touched started to get delivered. Some of the people were too afraid so they tried to run out of the building.)

Brice. You can run but you can't hide from God. Jezebel! You evil spirit of rebellion. I cast you out of my brothers and my sisters in the mighty name of Jesus.

(The people who were trying to run out of the church all fell to their faces and couldn't go any further. Yolanda was truly amazed by what was happening. She even forgot that the camera was rolling and didn't know how much time was left. Her cameramen were having difficulty staying composed, and most of her staff were trembling and shaking, while others were shouting and getting delivered.)

Brice. Somebody open up those exit doors. These demons don't seem to understand. I am not a son of Sceva. I am a child of the one, and only true God, and in the name of the Father, the Son, and the Holy Spirit. Demons get out!

(A young lady grabbed her Bible and touched a young man with it.)

Lady. You get out of him now! You will not keep him from me. I love him, and you can't have him.

(The man stood up and looked at the lady. He began to weep and then he hugged her, and they both began to praise and shout. Pastor Realton made his way back to the pulpit, and he noticed that Yolanda had a spirit next to her as well. He walked toward her with his Bible, and all of a sudden, Brice woke up from his coma. It had been seven months since he had slipped into the coma. During that time, Brice had been identified by his girlfriend, Trisha, who later gave up on him. She decided to go back to Troy, but before she did, she gave Brice sister a call, and his sister and some of his family from Houston came to be by his side. His niece and his nephew constantly prayed for him, and they always knew that he would come out of the coma because he was a fighter. Dr. Rivers and her good friend Dr. Washington were able to be there at the time. Apparently, together, they teamed up and was able to put a stop to the secret operation that Dr.

McGee had been trying to set up. After a while, Brice was able to tell everyone about his dream and all that he could remember before the coma. Dr. Washington's phone rang.)

Dr. Washington. Hi there, honey. I'm just back down here checking on Jamie's patient. He just came out of his coma recently. Okay, I will call you later. Love you too. Bye-bye.

Dr. Rivers. Stacey again? You two seem to be pretty happy together.

Dr. Washington. Yeah, we are.

Dr. Rivers. When do we get to meet?

Dr. Washington. About that, Jamie, I've been meaning to tell you something.

Dr. Rivers. And what that might be? You know what, don't even bother. I already know what you're going to say.

Dr. Washington. You do? When did you figure it out?

Dr. Rivers. Ever since you and I split up. I used to think that it was me or something that I did.

Dr. Washington. It was never you, Jamie. You are very smart, beautiful, and I always loved you. I just didn't have it in me to tell you. And now that Stacey and I are getting married, I feel like I need to tell you.

Dr. Rivers. You're getting married?

Dr. Washington. Yes, Jamie, Stacey and I are perfect for each other. And ever since he and I met. (Doc Rivers immediately cuts him off.)

Dr. Rivers. Wait a minute! Hold up one minute! I know that you just didn't stand there and tell me he and I…

Dr. Washington. I'm sorry, Jamie. I thought that you knew. I never meant to hurt you.

Dr. Rivers. Hurt me. Hurt me, Henry! The man that I fell in love with, the love of my life dumped me and left me hanging while I was thinking that he was just married to his work and didn't have the time to care about me or anyone else. And now I find out that you are getting married to a man. You left me because you were attracted to men? Men, Henry!

(Brice and his family couldn't help but notice that they were having a pretty heated conversation. Dr. Rivers looked over at Brice with tears falling from her eyes. They stared at each other for what seemed like eternity. Brice put his finger over his lips and just looked at her like saying, "It's okay." Dr. Rivers wiped her tears away from her eyes and looked at Dr. Washington.)

Dr. Rivers. Henry, I will always love you. Don't you worry about me. Everything will be just fine.

About the Author

Aubrey Scott is a man with a lot of ambition. He is the last of seven children. He was born and raised in New Orleans and lived in a very poor part of the city. He saw a lot of poverty and hard times while growing up, so having a dream and a way to achieve it was very important to him. He went to school and then joined the army, where he became a ranger in a special operations unit. After four years, he went to college but dropped out soon after. He worked a lot of jobs for the next twenty years and could never seem to get it together, until he decided to do what God said. He decided to use his gift of communicating through writing and talking to those who would listen. After doing so, he decided to write a book, hoping it could change the lives of many, especially his and his fourteen-year-old daughter Breeanna's. Now his goal is to do God's will and remain humble as God begins to direct him on his journey.